Chef Tim Creehan's

Flavors of the

GULF COAST

Tim Creehan, CEC

Tim Creehan
    Text copyright © 2000
    Photographs copyright © 2000

Illustrated and Designed by Denise Creehan © 2000

ISBN 0-9634545-1-X

Tim Creehan, C.E.C.   www.beachwalkcafe.com
Creehan's Market ®   www.grillplus.com
P.O. Box 1504   (888) 837-4735
Destin, Florida 32540   (850) 837-4735

First Edition, First Printing	1992	5,000 copies
Second Printing	1994	5,000 copies
Second Edition, First Printing	2000	5,000 copies

Printed in the USA by
WIMMER
The Wimmer Companies
Memphis
1-800-548-2537

Chef Tim Creehan has become one of the youngest and most accomplished Certified Executive Chefs in America.

Born in Hartford, Connecticut, Tim lived the majority of his childhood and young adult life in Baton Rouge, Louisiana.

At the young age of fifteen, Tim began his career in the culinary arts at Steak and Ale in Baton Rouge.

Chef Creehan's love of fine dining has garnered awards and acclaim from discriminating diners and fine chefs everywhere.

Chef Creehan studied under the esteemed Executive Chef Philippe Parola and advanced to the position of Executive Chef at Lafitte's Landing. Tim's tenure at Lafitte's vaulted this river-road dinner house into an internationally recognized, white-tablecloth restaurant.

Creehan was the Corporate Executive Chef at Ralph and Kacoo's Seafood Restaurant, which operated five establishments throughout Louisiana and presently is owned by Picadilly Cafeterias.

During the four years that Tim served as consulting chef for Country Skillet Catfish, a Con Agra Company, he was involved with recipe/product development and promotion.

Chef Creehan's accolades include awards in competitions sanctioned by the American Culinary Federation. He received Best of Show Award in the 1992 annual Emerald Coast Chef's Challenge. Tim was honored with the DiRoNa Award in 1997 and recognized as a Shining Star Chef by Cooking Light®'s Grandstand '99. He has been a member of the Great Chefs of America since 1989.

In March 2000, Chef Creehan was honored with a personal invitation to be the *chef de cuisine* at Amy Grant and Vince Gill's wedding reception for 500 guests. Tim showcased his culinary skills in this high profile venue which resulted in multimedia coverage including interviews in *People* Magazine and on the NBC television show EXTRA. He has cooked for celebrities Cybill Shepherd, Timothy Hutton and Catherine Crosby. He has appeared on TNN's *Cooking USA* with Merle Ellis and at New Orleans Riverwalk *Cookin' Cajun* Cooking School. Tim's famous cooking classes celebrate his natural teaching talents and present an opportunity to share his love for cooking. His volunteer participation in the *All Kinds of Art Culinary Program* for Destin middle school students and Harvest House's *Hope for the Holidays* reveal his commitment to the community and numerous charitable organizations.

Tim lives in Destin, Florida and is the owner and Executive Chef of Beach Walk Café on the Gulf of Mexico. He tirelessly explores ways to improve and simplify his culinary skills and his life.

The recipes in this book are designed to be easily prepared without much need for special equipment or ingredients. In these recipes as well as in all cookbooks, use the ingredients as a foundation and build recipes by improvising with your personal taste in mind. For instance, if a recipe seems interesting to you but you don't care for fish, substitute veal, chicken or beef. This substitution method can be applied to almost all recipes.

Approaching recipes with this in mind, you will begin to build confidence in your cooking ability and start the process of individual recipe development.

I strongly believe that there are few rules that apply to cooking. The one that I have made for myself to follow is that if it tastes great, it must be right!

The American Culinary Federation (ACF) is the largest professional organization of chefs in America. It is recognized by the international World Association of Cooks Societies (WACS).

The ACF founded its Educational Institute (ACFEI) in 1963 with the mission of providing quality assurance within the profession.

Since that time, the ACFEI has established nationally recognized education program accreditation (recognized by the United States Secretary of Education) and apprenticeship training (registered with the United States Department of Labor). In fact, these are the only programs available in the United States that carry these formal recognitions and registrations.

It is vital to the culinary profession that such talented chefs as Tim Creehan, CEC have taken such a vital role in the development and implementation of these programs. It will keep American chefs on the leading edge of the culinary profession worldwide. The global culinary community is observing the lead of the ACF and gaining guidance from our innovative programs. Already, American chefs have risen to world championship status in international culinary competition. We are poised to pass on this success to future generations.

The future of the Culinary Arts is in the hands of such industry leaders as Chef Creehan. His involvement through such projects as this excellent cookbook, which will serve as a valuable resource, will insure our place at the forefront of creativity. This volume will serve as a valuable addition to your library. When utilizing this work please pay close attention to Chef Creehan's imaginative use of flavor combinations and his flare for the unusual. The recipes demonstrate his comprehensive understanding of taste. I am sure you will enjoy the fruits of his labor.

Louis F. Jesowskek, CEC, AAC
American Culinary Federation Louisiana State Governor

Memory

In memory of Chef and Uncle John Vignone. My Uncle John was an inspiration to me many years ago, when I first decided to pursue my culinary arts career. He was a graduate of the Culinary Institute of America and worked many years achieving his many impressive goals.

I recall John telling me to document my recipes and publish a cookbook. This cookbook is a realization of his recommendation. It is published to perpetuate Uncle John's memory and his wish to provide readers with a way to truly enjoy the art of fine cooking.

Chef's Grill Plus®, a versatile non-stick cooking sauce, was introduced and patented in 1994. I created this revolutionary seasoning sauce to simplify the fine art of grilling fish, seafood, meat, chicken and vegetables. I recommend using Chef's Grill Plus® with any recipe that calls for dripping, dredging or brushing with oil. Chef's Grill Plus® may be substituted when a marinade is used in combination with seasonings. For example, the old method of brushing foods with butter or olive oil (see Grilled Trigger Fish, page 173 and Assorted Grilled Vegetables, page 82) may be replaced with an application of Chef's Grill Plus®.

Chef's Grill Plus® can also be used for baking, pan sautéing, broiling, roasting, as a condiment, a seasoned milk wash for frying, or tossed in with hot boiled seafood for that extra zip. Mixed with sour cream, Chef's Grill Plus® produces a tasty dip. Combined with smoked tuna and cream cheese, tossed with penne pasta, Chef's Grill Plus® creates a great salad.

Chef's Grill Plus®
- Quick and easy — just brush it on
- Low fat, low sodium, low cholesterol
- Eliminate food from sticking to cooking surfaces
- No smoke, no annoying flare-ups when grilling
- Create beautiful grill marks and appetizing color
- Economical - only cents per serving
- Versatile - grill, bake, pan sauté, broil, roast, fry, dip and zip!
- Guaranteed consistent flavor
- Four flavors — Original, Lemon Pepper, Fiery Hot Habanero and Mesquite Grill

Chef's Grill Plus® is available in 2-ounce trial size, 7-ounce retail containers, or one-half gallon food service container. Order forms may be found at the back of this cookbook. Sample packets are available by request. Visit our website www.grillplus.com.

For a *free* sample of **Chef's Grill Plus**®
check us out on our web page at www.grillplus.com

Questions or comments?
Call our toll free number: 1-888-457-4735

E-mail us: info@grillplus.com

Contents

Soups

Stocks

As an artist uses reds, yellows and blues for a base to create a world of rainbows, I employ stocks as an essential ingredient in most culinary creations. A strong foundation in the preparation of stocks is vital in order to create interesting sauces, flavorful consommés, gumbos and bisques.

Most basic stocks can be prepared from simple ingredients and will be used throughout this cookbook. These magically flavored liquids will enhance the most simple dish.

Chicken stock may be used to boil polenta, pasta, rice or risotto. Beef stock will sauté vegetables or baste meats. Fish and shrimp stocks flavor bisques or veloutés. Given the choice of flavorless water or an enriched stock, the use of stocks in all recipes is evident.

One of the greatest benefits of preparing stocks is that many of the ingredients used are those that are usually discarded. Onion tops and peelings, tomato skins and hulls, carcasses from roasted poultry, bones from fish and meat and the remains of chopped parsley and fresh herbs recycle nicely as stocks. Most stocks require forty-five minutes to twenty-four hours to prepare and can be kept frozen in small portions for future use.

Soups, simple or complex, must achieve a tasteful crescendo with a single pass over the palate. Great composers fill staffs with many notes and strive for one tone strong enough to stand alone. A soup should also challenge our taste with one complete flavor.

Soups keep well, so making one or two gallons at a time makes the effort worthwhile. Many quick, hot snacks or light lunches will follow. Everyone enjoys a great soup but many people are intimidated by them. With this varied collection, I know you will be making a lot of people very happy.

The following stock recipes will require an eight to ten gallon stock pot for a four to six gallon liquid yield. These recipes may be broken down somewhat, but since the preparation time is so long and the shelf life for most stocks is anywhere from two weeks refrigerated to one year frozen, it is beneficial to make them in large quantities.

The technique of browning bones will appear in some of the recipes. The purpose of this is to render the majority of the essence locked inside the marrow and also to obtain the deep rich color of a well prepared stock. The browning should be done in a short sided braising pan and at a temperature between 450 and 500 degrees.

The constant skimming of grease and the use of a slow rolling boil avoids a bitter tasting stock. If a stock is rapidly boiled and not skimmed, the waste and grease will be emulsified or fused into the finished product.

The use of strainers is an absolute must. A china cap, chinois, cheese cloth or paper filter is necessary to finish a stock properly. The absence of this step will produce a cloudy, particle-filled stock, not very attractive for sauce reductions and unacceptable for consommés.

The preparation of the vegetables or mirepoix, as well as the various herbs used for stocks is very simple. Wash and cut them into large coarse pieces. The skins of onions, garlic and carrots along with the leaves of celery and stems of herbs need not be removed.

It is almost impossible to overcook or over reduce a stock. As long as the stock is not burnt, water can always be added back to the pot and the reduction started again.

Veal Stock

4	pound	beef or veal bone
1	pound	meat scrap (optional)
1	cup	white flour
2	large	yellow onion
2	rib	celery
3	large	carrot
1	head	garlic
1	sprig	parsley
1	10 ounce can	whole peeled tomato
2	gallon	red wine
2	cup	white wine
2	tablespoon	whole thyme
2		bay leaf
1	teaspoon	black peppercorn

Procedure: • Crack the bones to expose the marrow. Lightly dust the bones
with white flour and brown with optional meat scraps.

Place the browned bones and vegetables, along with the remaining ingredients, in an 8 to 10 gallon stock pot filled with warm water approximately 4 inches from the top.

Bring the stock to a slow rolling boil for 12 to 24 hours skimming the grease constantly.

Remove the stock from the heat and strain through a medium sieve or china cap into a heavy bottom pot. The yield should be approximately half.

Reduce another 3 to 4 hours skimming the grease constantly. Add 2 cups of red wine and season with salt and white pepper.

After this volume has been reduced by half, strain the stock through a fine sieve or chinois and cool for storage.

Veal stock is the base sauce from which demi glace and glace de viande are formed. Demi glace or brown sauce is simply veal stock thickened with a blonde roux and the addition of tomato puree. This sauce sometimes is referred to as espanole. Roux (1 cup of butter and 1 cup of flour) with 3 tablespoons of tomato puree added to each gallon of veal stock forms a brown sauce. Glace de viande is veal stock reduced by 2/3 the original volume with the addition of 3 cups of red wine to each gallon of veal stock. Glace de viande is an intense, rich sauce which can be served with various meat dishes or used as a flavor enchancer for the base of many classical sauces.

Chicken Stock

4		chicken carcass
2	large	yellow onion
2	rib	celery
3	large	carrot
1	head	garlic
1	sprig	parsley
1	gallon	white wine
2	tablespoon	whole thyme
2		bay leaf
1	tablespoon	white pepper

Procedure:

- Place all of the ingredients in a 8 to 10 gallon stock pot. If the chicken carcasses are not from previously cooked chicken, add them to the stock raw.

  Fill the stock pot with warm water 4 inches from the top. Bring to a slow rolling boil for 2 hours skimming the grease constantly.

  Remove the stock from the heat, strain through a fine sieve or chinois and allow to cool. The yield should be approximately half.

Turkey Stock

This recipe is designed to utilize one Thanksgiving turkey carcass and its meat scraps.

1		turkey carcass and meat scrap
1	large	yellow onion
1	rib	celery
2	large	carrot
1	head	garlic
1	sprig	parsley
4	cup	white wine
2		bay leaf
1	tablespoon	whole thyme
1	teaspoon	white pepper

Procedure: • Place all of the ingredients in a 4 to 5 gallon stock pot filled with warm water 4 inches from the top.

Bring the stock to a slow rolling boil for 1 to 2 hours skimming the grease constantly.

Remove the stock from the heat, strain through a fine sieve or chinois and allow to cool. The yield should be approximately half.

Fish Stock

6	pound	fish bone (no head)
1	cup	olive oil
2	large	yellow onion
2	rib	celery
3	large	carrot
1	sprig	parsley
1	cup	sherry
4	cup	white wine
1	tablespoon	whole thyme
3	whole	clove
3		bay leaf
1	tablespoon	black peppercorn

Procedure: • Heat the olive oil in a 4 to 5 gallon stock pot and add the fish bones. Cook until bones and meat have turned white.

Add all of the remaining ingredients and fill the stock pot with warm water 4 inches from the top. Boil for 1 hour skimming the oil constantly.

Remove the stock from the heat, strain through a fine sieve or chinois and allow to cool.

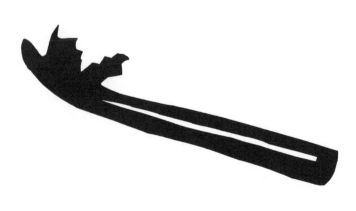

Shrimp Stock

10	pound	shrimp shell (no head)
2	large	yellow onion
2	rib	celery
2	large	carrot
1	head	garlic
1	sprig	parsley
4	cup	white wine
1	cup	sherry
1	cup	tomato puree
1	tablespoon	coriander seed
1	tablespoon	whole thyme
3		bay leaf
1	tablespoon	white pepper

Procedure: ▪ *Place all of the ingredients in a 4 to 5 gallon stock pot and fill with warm water 4 inches from the top. Bring the stock to a slow rolling boil for 1 to 2 hours.*

Remove the stock from the heat, strain through a fine sieve or chinois and allow to cool.

Lobster Stock

10		Maine lobster shell and head, chopped
1	cup	olive oil
2	large	yellow onion
2	rib	celery
3	large	carrot
2	head	garlic
1	sprig	parsley
4	cup	white wine
1	cup	sherry
2	cup	brandy
3	tablespoon	whole thyme
2	tablespoon	black peppercorn
3		bay leaf
1	cup	tomato puree

Procedure: • Heat the olive oil in a large braising pan and add the chopped lobster shells along with the vegetables. Sauté until the vegetables and shells are browned lightly.

Flambe with brandy and transfer all of the ingredients to an 8 gallon stock pot.

Add the white wine, sherry, tomato puree and all of the remaining ingredients and fill the stock pot 4 inches from the top with warm water.

Boil the stock for 4 hours skimming the oil constantly.

Remove the stock from the heat, strain through a fine sieve or chinois and allow to cool.

Vegetable Stock

There are situations with particular food preparations when the products necessary to produce a meat, poultry or seafood stock are not readily available. A simple vegetable stock is a good substitute in this situation. Whenever a recipe calls for a stock and one is not available, a vegetable stock is certainly more flavorful than water.

1/2	cup	olive oil
4	large	yellow onion
4	rib	celery
3	large	carrot
2	head	garlic
3		tomato (canned whole or fresh)
2	sprig	parsley
2	tablespoon	whole thyme
2		bay leaf
1	tablespoon	black peppercorn
2	cup	white wine

Procedure: • Heat the olive oil in a 4 to 5 gallon stock pot and sauté the vegetables until lightly brown. Flambe with white wine and fill the stock pot 4 inches from the top with warm water.

Bring the stock to a rapid boil for 1 hour and remove from the heat. Strain through a fine sieve or chinois and allow to cool.

Duck Stock

This stock recipe works well with all types of game. Simply substitute the duck carcasses with bones from the particular type of game you are working with.

8		duck carcass (meat scrap optional)
3	large	yellow onion
2	rib	celery
3	large	carrot
3	head	garlic
1	sprig	parsley
4	cup	red wine
1	cup	white wine
2	cup	whole tomato
2	tablespoon	black peppercorn
2	tablespoon	whole thyme
3		bay leaf

Procedure:

- *Brown the duck bones in a 450° oven.*

Place the bones and all of the remaining ingredients in a 8 to 10 gallon stock pot and fill with warm water 4 inches from the top.

Bring the stock to a slow rolling boil for 6 hours skimming the grease constantly. Remove the stock from the heat and strain through a fine sieve or chinois and allow to cool.

Lamb Stock

10	pound	lamb bone
3	pound	beef or veal bone
1	pound	bacon, fried
3	large	yellow onion
2	rib	celery
3	large	carrot
2	head	garlic
1	sprig	parsley
1	cup	tomato puree
2	cup	red wine
2	cup	white wine
3	tablespoon	whole thyme
2	tablespoon	black peppercorn
3		bay leaf

Procedure: ■ Brown the lamb and beef bones in a 450° oven.

Transfer the browned bones, fried bacon and all of the remaining ingredients to a 8 to 10 gallon stock pot and fill with warm water 4 inches from the top.

Bring the stock to a slow rolling boil for 12 hours skimming the grease constantly.

Remove the stock from the heat, strain through a fine sieve or chinois and allow to cool.

Roasted Sweet Pepper Soup

15		red or gold sweet pepper
1	quart	chicken stock
1	tablespoon	garlic, chopped
3	tablespoon	tomato paste
12	large	basil leaf, chopped
3	tablespoon	olive oil
	to taste	salt
	to taste	crushed red pepper

*Requested by
GOURMET magazine*

Procedure: ■ Roast the sweet peppers over an open flame until the skins are completely charred. Place the peppers in a brown paper bag and allow to cool for 15 minutes.

Remove the sweet peppers from the bag and rinse the charred skins off under cool running water. Remove the stems and seeds from the peppers and puree in a food processor or blender.

Heat the chicken stock in a heavy bottom pot and add the pureed peppers, garlic, and tomato paste. Bring to a slow boil for 25 minutes.

Season to taste with salt and crushed red pepper. Finish with olive oil and basil shortly before serving.

Serves 10

Seafood Bisque

1	stick	butter
1/2		onion, diced
1	tablespoon	garlic, chopped
1/2	rib	celery, diced
1	cup	Italian plum tomato, crushed
1/2	cup	white flour
1/4	cup	sherry
1	cup	white wine
2	cup	heavy cream
1	quart	milk
2	ounce	scallop
2	ounce	crawfish tail
4	ounce	baby shrimp
2	ounce	crabmeat
1	cup	clam (with juice)
10	ounce	fish, diced
1	teaspoon	lemon juice
1/2	bunch	green onion, chopped
1	teaspoon	paprika
2	tablespoon	basil, chopped
	to taste	salt
	to taste	black pepper
	to taste	cayenne pepper

Procedure:

• Melt the butter in a heavy bottom pot and sauté the onions, garlic, celery and tomatoes for 10 minutes.

Stir in the flour until all is incorporated.

Slowly add the sherry, white wine, cream and milk. Stirring continuously. Bring to a slow boil.

Add all of the seafood ingredients, lemon juice, green onions and paprika. Bring back to a slow boil.

Simmer for 20 to 30 minutes, add the basil and season to taste with salt, black pepper and cayenne pepper.
Serves 12

Corn and Crab Bisque

2	stick	butter
1	large	yellow onion, chopped
2	tablespoon	garlic, chopped
2	14-1/2 oz. can	corn (1 cream style, 1 regular)
1/2	cup	flour
3	cup	chicken stock
1	quart	heavy cream
1/2	pound	lump crabmeat
1	bunch	green onion, chopped
	to taste	salt
	to taste	black pepper

Procedure: ▣ *Melt the butter in heavy bottom pot and sauté the chopped onions, garlic and corn for 5 minutes.*

Stir in the flour until all is incorporated. Slowly blend in the chicken stock stirring continuously.

Bring this mixture to a slow boil for 25 minutes. Add the heavy cream and season to taste with salt and black pepper. Finish with green onions and jumbo lump crabmeat.
Serves 10

Hot and Sour Soup

2	quart	chicken stock
1	cup	soy sauce
1	cup	rice vinegar
3/4	cup	sugar
2	tablespoon	garlic, chopped
1	tablespoon	ginger root, chopped
1	tablespoon	crushed red pepper
1	cup	Napa cabbage, shredded
1		carrot, julienned
1/2		red sweet pepper, julienned
1	can	bamboo shoot, julienned
1		red onion, julienned
4		egg, whipped
1/2	cup	water
1/4	cup	corn starch
2	teaspoon	sesame oil

Procedure: • *Bring the chicken stock, soy sauce, rice vinegar, sugar, garlic, ginger and crushed red pepper to a slow boil.*

Add the cabbage, carrots, red sweet pepper, bamboo shoots and red onion. Bring back to a boil.

Blend the corn starch and water together. Slowly add to the boiling soup stirring continuously until desired thickness.

Turn off the heat. Add the sesame oil and slowly blend in whipped eggs to achieve the egg drop effect.
Serves 10

Seafood Gumbo

2	stick	butter
1	cup	canola oil
2	large	yellow onion, diced
1		bell pepper, diced
4	rib	celery, diced
2	tablespoon	garlic, chopped
2	cup	white flour
2	cup	tomato, diced
3	quart	shrimp or chicken stock
2	cup	fish, diced
1	cup	baby shrimp
1	cup	oyster (with liquor)
1	cup	crabmeat
2	cup	okra
2	ounce	Kitchen Bouquet®
1	bunch	green onion, chopped
	to taste	salt
	to taste	black pepper
	to taste	cayenne pepper

Procedure: • *Heat the butter and oil in a heavy bottom pot and sauté the onions, bell pepper, celery and garlic for 5 minutes.*

Stir in the flour until all is incorporated. Slowly add the stock and tomato stirring continuously. Bring to a boil.

Reduce to a simmer and add all of the remaining ingredients except the green onions. Cook for 45 minutes.

Season to taste with salt, black pepper and cayenne pepper. Garnish with chopped green onions. Serve over steamed rice.
Serves 15

Crawfish and Mushroom Velouté

This soup can be prepared without the crawfish for a great mushroom soup.

2	stick	butter
1	large	yellow onion, diced
3	pound	mushroom
1	tablespoon	garlic, chopped
1	cup	white flour
1/4	cup	sherry
2	tablespoon	lemon juice
1	quart	chicken stock
1	quart	heavy cream
1	pound	crawfish tail
	to taste	salt
	to taste	white pepper

Procedure:

- Wash the mushrooms and puree in a food processor.

  Melt the butter in a heavy bottom pot and sauté the garlic, onions and mushrooms for 5 to 7 minutes.

  Stir in the flour until all is incorporated. Slowly blend in all of the remaining ingredients stirring continuously.

  Bring to a slow boil, reduce to a simmer for 30 minutes and season to taste with salt and white pepper.
  Serves 12

Chicken and Andouille Gumbo

1	whole	chicken (may substitute duck)
1	cup	canola oil
2	large	yellow onion, diced
1		bell pepper, diced
3	rib	celery, diced
1	tablespoon	garlic, chopped

10	ounce	tomato, diced
1	cup	white flour
1	pound	andouille sausage, sliced
1/4	cup	Kitchen Bouquet®
3	quart	water
1	bunch	green onion, chopped
	to taste	salt
	to taste	black pepper
	to taste	cayenne pepper

Procedure:

• *Boil the chicken in the water for 25 minutes. Remove the chicken and allow it to cool. Debone and dice the chicken meat. Reserve the water.*

Heat the oil in a heavy bottom pot and sauté the onions, bell peppers, celery, garlic, tomatoes and andouille sausage for 5 minutes.

Stir in the flour until all is incorporated. Slowly add the water stirring continuously and bring to a slow boil for 45 minutes.

Add the Kitchen Bouquet,® diced chicken meat and chopped green onions. Reduce to a simmer for 30 minutes.

Season to taste with salt, black pepper and cayenne pepper. Serve over steamed rice.

Serves 12

Black Bean Soup with Pico de Gallo and Sour Cream

1/2	cup	canola oil
1	large	onion, diced
1	rib	celery, diced
2		carrot, diced
2	tablespoon	garlic, chopped
2	cup	black bean
1	gallon	water
2	tablespoon	ketchup
1	tablespoon	oregano
	to taste	black pepper
3	tablespoon	brown sugar
2	cup	sour cream
1/4	pound	bacon, fried and chopped
	to taste	salt

• *Pico de Gallo*

1		tomato, diced
1		jalapeno, diced
1/2	large	yellow onion, diced
1/2	bunch	cilantro, chopped
1	teaspoon	salt
1	tablespoon	white vinegar

Procedures:

• *Soup*
Heat the oil in a heavy bottom pot and sauté the onions, celery, carrots and garlic for 5 minutes.

Add all of the remaining ingredients except for the salt and pepper. Bring to a slow boil for 3 hours.

Season to taste with salt and pepper. Add additional water if necessary to adjust consistency. Garnish each serving with sour cream and pico de gallo.

• *Pico de Gallo*
Blend all ingredients in a mixing bowl and chill.
Serves 12

Shrimp Bisque

2	quart	shrimp stock
1	cup	white wine
1	cup	blonde roux
1	cup	tomato paste
2	cup	heavy cream
1	pound	baby shrimp
	to taste	sherry
	to taste	salt
	to taste	white pepper

Procedures:

• *Blonde Roux*
Blend equal parts of butter and flour over heat. Cook 2 minutes.

• *Soup*
In a heavy bottom pot, bring the shrimp stock and wine to a slow boil for 25 minutes.

Blend in the blonde roux and tomato paste stirring continuously. Return to a slow boil for 45 minutes.

Add all of the remaining ingredients. Cook an additional 10 minutes and season to taste with salt and white pepper.
Serves 12

Leek and Potato Soup

2	stick	butter
4	cup	leek or onion, chopped
3	cup	potato, diced
1	tablespoon	garlic, chopped
3/4	cup	white flour
2	quart	chicken stock
2	cup	heavy cream
	to taste	salt
	to taste	white pepper

Procedure: • *Heat the butter in a heavy bottom pot and sauté the leeks, potatoes and garlic for 5 minutes.*

Stir in the flour until all is incorporated. Slowly add the chicken stock and heavy cream stirring continuously. Bring to a slow boil for 30 minutes.

Remove half the soup from the pot. Transfer to a food processor and puree. Return the pureed soup to the remaining soup and season to taste with salt and white pepper.
Serves 12

Lentil Bean Soup

1/4	pound	bacon, chopped
1	large	yellow onion, diced
2		carrot, diced fine
2	tablespoon	garlic, chopped
12	ounce	Italian plum tomato, pureed
2	quart	veal stock
3/4	cup	tomato puree
2	quart	water
1	pound	lentil bean
2	tablespoon	oregano
2	tablespoon	basil
2		bay leaf
1	cup	romano cheese, grated
1/4	cup	olive oil
	to taste	salt
	to taste	black pepper

Procedure:

- *In a heavy bottom pot, fry the bacon and sauté the onions, carrots and garlic for 5 minutes.*

Add the tomatoes, veal stock, tomato puree, water and bring to a boil. Add the lentil beans, oregano, basil, bay leaves, romano cheese and bring to a slow boil for 1 hour.

Season to taste with salt and black pepper. Finish with olive oil.
Serves 12

Oyster and Artichoke Soup

2	stick	butter
1	large	yellow onion, diced
2	rib	celery
1		bell pepper, diced
1	tablespoon	garlic, chopped
2	can	artichoke heart, quartered (reserve liquid)
2	cup	white flour
2	cup	oyster (with liquor)
1	cup	white wine
3	quart	chicken stock
2	cup	heavy cream
3		green onion, chopped

to taste	salt
to taste	black pepper
to taste	cayenne pepper

Procedure: • *Melt the butter in heavy bottom pot and sauté the onions, celery, bell pepper, garlic and artichoke hearts for 10 minutes.*

Stir in the flour until all is incorporated. Slowly add the white wine, chicken stock and cream stirring continuously. Bring to a slow boil for 25 minutes.

Add the oysters with liquor, liquid reserved from the artichoke hearts, green onions and season to taste with salt, black pepper and cayenne pepper. Simmer for at least 30 minutes.
Serves 15

Tomato, Basil and Cream Soup

1/2	cup	olive oil
1	large	yellow onion, diced
2	tablespoon	garlic, chopped
4	28 oz. can	Italian plum tomato, peeled
10	ounce	chicken stock
3	cup	heavy cream
1/2	cup	basil, chopped
1/2	cup	Romano cheese, grated
	to taste	salt
	to taste	black pepper

Procedure: • *Heat the olive oil in a heavy bottom pot and sauté the onions, garlic and tomatoes for 10 minutes.*

Add the chicken stock and bring to a boil. Transfer to a food processor and puree. Return to the pot and add the heavy cream, chopped basil and bring back to a slow boil.

Season to taste with salt, black pepper and Romano cheese.
Serves 12

Louisiana Turtle Soup

1	cup	sherry
1	cup	white wine
1	quart	veal stock
1	quart	chicken stock
1	pound	turtle meat, cleaned
1	large	yellow onion, quartered
1	rib	celery, chopped
1/2		bell pepper, quartered
1	large	carrot, chopped
1	tablespoon	garlic, chopped
1		bay leaf
1	tablespoon	thyme
2	tablespoon	basil
2	tablespoon	oregano
3/4	cup	tomato puree
1/4	cup	parsley, chopped
3		egg, boiled and chopped
	to taste	salt
	to taste	black pepper

Procedure:

• *Place all of the ingredients, except eggs, parsley, tomato puree and seasonings in a large, heavy bottom pot. Boil for 45 minutes.*

Pour the stock through a strainer. Reserve all of the solid ingredients and puree in a food processor. Return to the stock.

Bring the soup to a slow boil for 25 minutes, add the tomato puree, eggs and parsley. Season to taste with salt and black pepper. Thicken with a roux if desired. (See recipe page 30.)
Serves 12

Tuscan Style Tomato Soup

1/3	cup	olive oil
1	tablespoon	rosemary, chopped
1/2	loaf	French bread, stale and diced
1	cup	yellow onion, diced
2	tablespoon	garlic, chopped
1/3	cup	tomato paste
2	quart	Italian plum tomato, peeled and diced

3	cup	veal stock
1/2	cup	basil, chopped
3	tablespoon	olive oil
	to taste	salt
	to taste	black pepper

Procedure: • *Heat the olive oil in a heavy bottom pot and sauté the onions, rosemary and garlic for 5 minutes. Add the diced tomatoes, tomato paste and simmer for 20 minutes.*

Add the veal stock, bread and basil. Transfer half of the soup to a food processor and puree.

Return the pureed soup to the pot and simmer for 20 minutes. Season to taste with salt, black pepper. Finish with olive oil.
Serves 12

Potato, Corn and Andouille Soup

1	stick	butter
1	large	yellow onion, diced
2	tablespoon	garlic, chopped
1/4	pound	andouille sausage, chopped
2	14-1/2 oz. can	corn
3	large	potato, diced
2	quart	chicken stock
1/2	cup	green onions, chopped

Procedure: • *Melt the butter in a heavy bottom pot and sauté the onions, garlic, corn and andouille sausage for 10 minutes.*

Add the potatoes and chicken stock. Bring to a slow boil for 45 minutes.

Season to taste with salt and black pepper and finish with the chopped green onions. Puree a portion of the soup for texture if desired.
Serves 12

Appetizers

The appetizer is one of the most important components of a wonderful dining experience and the first impression of things to come for the dining guest. A flavorsome, artistically presented appetizer will whet the appetite through all the senses. Appetizers are invaluable for inspiring confidence and creating anticipation for the guest.

The preparation of appetizers is an exciting challenge. The final preparation stage for most appetizers requires no more than five to seven minutes.

Appetizers presented in this section vary from goat cheese stuffed Roma tomatoes to homemade, grilled duck sausage, served with sweet mustard.

When preparing appetizers, I enjoy using a wide variety of cheeses, as well as light frying. Most cheeses are appreciated in small servings due to their rich quality. Frying, with the use of canola oil or other unsaturated cooking oils, also lends itself to moderate use. When frying, always be aware of the "smoke point" of an oil. Certain oils tolerate higher temperatures and have a longer life after heating.

Cold appetizers are gaining in popularity. Thinly sliced smoked salmon, carpaccios, seafood and meats are easily prepared, attractive, light and naturally flavorful. Always use extra virgin olive oil in appetizer preparation.

Experiment with mixing and matching, creative presentation and unique foods in the preparation of appetizers. A lasting impression of the entire dinner is often the result of a clever appetizer.

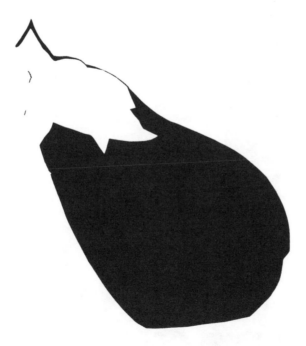

Eggplant Medallions with Jumbo Lump Crabmeat

▣ Hollandaise Sauce

1	stick	butter
2		egg yolk
1	tablespoon	lemon juice
1	shot	Tabasco®
1/4	cup	white wine

▣ Meuniere Sauce

1/2	cup	veal stock
1/2	cup	white wine
2	tablespoon	lemon juice
2	stick	butter, chipped

▣ Eggplant Medallions

1		eggplant
2		egg
1/2	cup	milk
		corn flour
1/2	pound	jumbo lump crabmeat
1/4	cup	butter, melted
1		green onion, chopped
2	teaspoon	lemon juice
	to taste	salt
	to taste	white pepper

Procedures:

▣ Hollandaise Sauce

Melt the butter. Blend the egg yolks, lemon juice and Tabasco® in a mixing bowl.

Flambe the white wine and pour it into the egg yolk mixture.

Whisk the egg yolk mixture over a double boiler until firm peaks form. Remove the eggs from the heat and whisk in the room temperature melted butter.

▣ Meuniere Sauce

Reduce the veal stock, white wine and lemon juice in a sauce pot to half the original volume.

Remove from the heat and whisk in the cool butter chips until all of the butter is incorporated.

• *Eggplant Medallions*
Preheat a deep fryer to 350°. Peel the eggplant and slice into 1/4 inch thick medallions.

Prepare an eggwash by blending the milk and eggs. Dip the medallions into the eggwash and then into the corn flour.

Fry the eggplant medallions until golden brown.

Sauté the crabmeat in the melted butter with the green onions and lemon juice. Season to taste with salt and white pepper.

Place the meuniere sauce on the base of 4 dinner plates. Place the eggplant medallions in the center of the plates topped with the sautéed lump crabmeat and finished with hollandaise sauce.
Serves 4

Crispy Fried Calamari with Remoulade Sauce

1	pound	baby squid, cleaned
2	cup	white flour
2	tablespoon	black pepper
1	teaspoon	cayenne pepper
1	teaspoon	granulated garlic
1	tablespoon	salt

• *Remoulade Sauce*

1	cup	mayonnaise
1/4	cup	Creole mustard
2	tablespoon	horseradish
1	tablespoon	red wine vinegar

Procedures:

• *Remoulade Sauce*
Blend all of the ingredients thoroughly in a mixing bowl.

• *Calamari*
Preheat a deep fryer to 375°.

Cut the cleaned squid in 3/4 inch segments and toss in the flour seasoned with salt, granulated garlic, black pepper and cayenne pepper. Shaking off all the excess flour.

Deep fry the calamari for 3 to 5 minutes. Serve immediately with the prepared remoulade sauce.
Serves 6

Grilled Sea Scallops, Southwestern Salsa, Lemon Butter Sauce

20		jumbo sea scallop
		olive oil
	to taste	salt
	to taste	white pepper

• Southwestern Salsa

1		tomato
1/2		red onion
1/2		jalapeno
1/2	bunch	cilantro
1/2		yellow sweet pepper
	to taste	salt
1	ounce	white vinegar
1	teaspoon	garlic, chopped

• Lemon Butter Sauce

1/2	cup	heavy cream
2	ounce	lemon juice
1	ounce	white wine
1	tablespoon	chive, chopped
1	tablespoon	garlic, chopped
1	stick	butter
	to taste	salt
	to taste	white pepper

Procedures:

• Southwestern Salsa
Dice all of the ingredients and blend thoroughly. Refrigerate.

• Lemon Butter Sauce
Reduce all of the ingredients except butter in a heavy sauce pot to half the original volume.

Slice the butter into chips and whisk into the reduced sauce stirring continuously until all butter is melted.

• Scallops
Brush the scallops with olive oil and season to taste with salt and white pepper. Grill the scallops, medium to medium well and serve with the prepared Southwestern salsa and lemon butter sauce.
Serves 4

Chicken and Poblano Quesadillas

8	10 inch	flour tortilla
1	pound	monterey jack cheese, grated
1	pound	cheddar cheese, grated
1	cup	chicken, cooked and sliced
2	tablespoon	poblano pepper, roasted and diced
1	cup	sour cream
1	large	tomato, diced
1		red onion, diced
1/4	cup	cilantro, chopped

Procedure:

▪ *Roast the poblano peppers over an open flame until the skins are completely charred. Rinse the peppers under cool running water to remove the skins. Chop and set aside.*

Place the tortillas on a sheet pan, top half with monterey jack cheese and poblano peppers. Top the remaining half with cheddar cheese and sliced chicken.

Place the tortillas under a broiler until the cheese has melted. Place the 2 opposite sides together and broil each side until brown and crisp.

Cut each quesadilla into 8 equal sections and garnish with sour cream, tomato, red onion and cilantro.
Serves 4

Eggplant Lasagna

▪ *Marinara Sauce*

4	cup	Italian plum tomato, peeled (with juice)
1/4	cup	olive oil
1/2	large	yellow onion, diced
4	clove	garlic, chopped
1/3	cup	tomato paste
1/2	cup	romano cheese, grated
1/2	cup	basil, chopped
	to taste	black pepper

· *Lasagna*

1	large	eggplant
18	ounce	goat cheese
6	ounce	mozzarella

Procedures: · *Marinara Sauce*

In a sauce pot, sauté the onions and garlic in olive oil for 5 minutes. Pass the tomatoes through a food mill, discard the pulp and add to the onions and garlic.

Bring to a slow boil. Add the tomato paste, black pepper, romano cheese and basil. Simmer for 30 minutes and adjust seasonings.

· *Lasagna*

Cut the eggplant into 1/8 inch slices lengthwise, skin on. Fry the eggplant in hot oil until soft and place on paper towels to absorb the excess oil.

Line the bottom of a 9x7 inch cake pan with eggplant slices. Top this layer evenly with half of the goat cheese. Repeat this step with the remaining eggplant and goat cheese to form a second layer.

Top the lasagna with marinara sauce and grated mozzarella. Bake in a 450° oven for 20 minutes. Allow to cool and cut into 2 inch squares. Reheat and serve with the additional marinara sauce.

Serves 8

Three Cheese Baked Oysters

32		oyster on the half shell
1	tablespoon	olive oil
1/4	cup	proscuitto, chopped
1	teaspoon	garlic, chopped
1/2	cup	mozzarella cheese, grated
1	cup	fontina cheese, grated
1	cup	romano cheese, grated
1/2	cup	heavy cream
1	tablespoon	Crystal® hot sauce
3/4	cup	bread crumb

Procedure: • Sauté the garlic and proscuitto in the olive oil for 3 minutes.

Add the heavy cream, fontina cheese, romano cheese and hot sauce. Simmer until all of the cheese has melted. Remove from the heat and allow to cool.

Sprinkle each oyster with grated mozzarella cheese, 1 ounce of the cheese sauce and bread crumbs. Bake in a 450°oven for 8 minutes.
Serves 4

Marinated Crab Claws

1	pound	crab claw
1/2	cup	olive oil
1/2	cup	red wine vinegar
3	tablespoon	Worcestershire sauce
1	bunch	green onion
1/2	rib	celery
1/2	bunch	parsley
4	clove	garlic
1/4	cup	green olive
	to taste	salt
	to taste	black pepper

Procedure: • Place all of the ingredients except the crab claws in a food processor and puree. Chill for at least 2 hours.

Arrange the crab claws on a plate and top with the marinade.
Serves 4

Garlic Crostini with Tomatoes and Mozzarella

16	1/4 inch slice	French bread crouton
1/3	cup	olive oil
2	tablespoon	garlic, chopped
1/2	cup	mozzarella, diced
2	large	tomato, diced
3	tablespoon	basil, chopped
	to taste	salt
	to taste	black pepper

Procedure: · *Toast the croutons until brown and crispy. Brush each crostini with olive oil and garlic.*

In a mixing bowl, blend the mozzarella, tomatoes, basil, salt and black pepper. Let stand for 15 minutes.

Top each crostini with the tomato mixture and serve immediately.
Serves 4

Crispy Kung Pao Oysters

32		oyster on the half shell
2	cup	corn flour
1		red onion, sliced paper thin
1	tablespoon	poppy seed
1	teaspoon	ginger, chopped
2	teaspoon	garlic, chopped
1	tablespoon	sugar
2	tablespoon	sherry
1/4	cup	oyster sauce (prepared oriental sauce)
1	tablespoon	rice vinegar
1/4	cup	soy sauce
1/4	cup	water
2	tablespoon	green onion, chopped
	to taste	crushed red pepper
1	tablespoon	corn starch

Procedure: · *Place the ginger, garlic, sugar, sherry, soy sauce, oyster sauce, rice vinegar and green onions in a sauté pan. Bring to a slow boil.*

Blend the corn starch with the water and add to the sauce. Bring the sauce back to a slow boil. Season to taste with red pepper and set aside.

Preheat a deep fryer to 375˚. Remove the oysters from the half shell and dredge in the corn flour. Fry the oysters until very crisp, approximately 4 minutes.

Place the fried oysters back on the half shell and top each oyster with 1 teaspoon of sauce, sliced red onion and sprinkle with poppy seeds.
Serves 4

Country Terrine

6	1/8 inch	pork chop (fatty cut preferred)
8	ounce	veal
10		chicken liver
1	head	garlic, peeled
1	large	yellow onion, diced fine
2	cup	port wine
1/2	cup	veal stock
2	tablespoon	sugar
11	strip	bacon
	to taste	salt
	to taste	black pepper
	to taste	thyme
	to taste	cayenne pepper

Procedure:

• Finely puree the pork, veal, 4 chicken livers and garlic in a food processor.

Sauté the onions with the port wine, sugar and veal stock for 5 minutes. Blend the 2 mixtures together and season to taste. Check the seasoning by cooking a small portion of the terrine mixture.

Preheat an oven to 350°.

Line a standard terrine mold with the bacon slices; the ends of the bacon will hang over the edges of the mold. Fill the lined mold half full with the terrine mixture, line the remaining chicken livers end to end down the center of the terrine and cover with the remaining terrine mixture.

Fold the bacon edges over the top of the prepared terrine. Place the mold in a pan with at least 2 inches of water. Cook the terrine for 1 hour.

Turn off the oven and allow the terrine to cool to room temperature in the oven. Refrigerate for 6 hours, remove from the mold and slice.
Serves 10

Grilled Japanese Eggplant with Baked Goat Cheese

4	medium	Japanese eggplant
8	1 ounce	goat cheese, slice
1/2	cup	olive oil
	to taste	salt
	to taste	black pepper
1	portion	marinara sauce (see page 42)

Procedure:

● Prepare 1 portion of the marinara sauce. Preheat a grill surface for at least 15 minutes.

From the top of the eggplant cut 4 to 5 1/8 inch lengthwise slices leaving the top inch of the stem connected. This will allow the eggplant to form a fan shape.

Dip the fan shaped eggplant in olive oil and season with salt and black pepper. Grill the eggplant for 10 minutes or until very soft.

Place 2 slices of goat cheese on top of each grilled eggplant and heat the cheese under a broiler.

Transfer the eggplant to a plate and serve topped with the heated marinara sauce. Garnish with fresh basil.
Serves 4

Oyster Stuffed Mushrooms

1	stick	butter
24	select	oyster
24	mediun	mushroom
1/2	medium	yellow onion
1	rib	celery
1/2		bell pepper
3	clove	garlic
1	tablespoon	lemon juice
1/4	cup	sherry
1/2	cup	white wine
	to taste	salt
	to taste	black pepper

Procedure: • *Puree the onion, celery, bell pepper, garlic, white wine, sherry, and lemon juice in a food processor.*

In a sauté pan, melt the butter and sauté the mushroom caps with stems removed for 5 minutes. Add the pureed ingredients and sauté an additional 5 minutes.

Add the oysters and season to taste with salt and black pepper. Cook only until the oysters are firm. Serve the oysters in the mushroom caps topped with the sauce formed in the sauté pan.
Serves 4

Louisiana Crabcakes with Sauce Piquante

• Crabcakes

1	pound	jumbo lump crabmeat
3		egg
2		green onion, chopped
2	teaspoon	garlic, chopped
1	tablespoon	lemon juice
2	tablespoon	sherry
2	teaspoon	curry powder
1/4	cup	romano cheese, grated
4	cup	bread crumb
	to taste	salt
	to taste	cayenne pepper

• Sauce Piquante

1	tablespoon	butter
1/4	cup	onion, chopped
1/4	cup	celery, chopped
1/4	cup	bell pepper, chopped
2	clove	garlic, chopped
1	cup	tomato puree
1/2	cup	chicken stock
1/2		jalapeno, chopped
1/4	cup	green onion, chopped
	to taste	salt

Procedures: · *Sauce Piquante*
Sauté the onions, celery, bell pepper, jalapeno and garlic in the butter for 5 minutes.

Add the chicken stock, tomato puree, green onions and bring to a slow boil for 15 minutes. Season to taste with salt and keep hot.

· *Crabcakes*
Blend all of the crabcake ingredients in a mixing bowl. Mix together carefully avoiding breaking the crabmeat lumps.

Form into 2x2 inch square cakes 1/4 inch thick.

Sauté or grill the cakes until heated throughout and serve with the prepared sauce piquante.
Serves 8

Norwegian Smoked Salmon with Horseradish Sauce

1/2	pound	Norwegian smoked salmon, presliced
1	small	red onion, diced fine
1/4	cup	caper
1/4	cup	mayonnaise
2	tablespoon	horseradish
2	teaspoon	red wine vinegar

Procedure: · Blend the mayonnaise, horseradish and red wine vinegar together in a squeeze bottle.

Place 2 ounces of the smoked salmon on each plate and garnish with the horseradish sauce, capers and onions.

Serve with fresh lemon and some form of crisp bread or prepared wafers.
Serves 4

Beef Sirloin Carpaccio

12	ounce	sirloin strip
1/4	cup	olive oil
2	tablespoon	green peppercorn
1	cup	romano cheese
2		sweet red pepper
	to taste	black pepper

Procedure:

• *Trim the sirloin strip of all excess fat and place in a freezer wrapped in clear wrap for 15 minutes. (This will make thinly slicing the beef much easier.)*

Roast the sweet peppers over an open flame until the skins are completely charred. Place the peppers in a brown paper bag for 15 minutes and allow to cool. Rinse the peppers under cool running water to remove the skins.

Remove the stems and seeds and julienne the peppers.

Slice the sirloin paper thin on a meat slicer and cover the base of 4 large dinner plates. If a meat slicer is not available, hand slice the meat as thin as possible, place between to 2 pieces of clear wrap and pound paper thin with a meat hammer.

Shave the romano cheese with a vegetable peeler on top of each carpaccio and drizzle with the olive oil. Garnish with pepper-corns, sweet peppers and fresh ground black pepper.
Serves 4

Baby Escargot in Mushroom Caps

20	small	snail
20	medium	mushroom
2	stick	butter
2	tablespoon	sundried tomato, chopped
3	tablespoon	garlic, chopped
1/2	cup	parsley, chopped
2	teaspoon	lemon juice
	to taste	black pepper

Procedure: • *Remove the stems from the mushrooms and wash. Melt the butter in a large sauté pan and sauté the mushroom caps for 5 minutes.*

Add all of the remaining ingredients and sauté for an additional 5 minutes. Season to taste with black pepper.

Serve the sautéed escargot in the mushroom caps topped with the sundried tomato and garlic butter sauce formed in the pan.
Serves 4

Scallops with Provencale Sauce

20		jumbo sea scallop
1	stick	butter
2	tablespoon	garlic, chopped
2		tomato, peeled and diced
1/4	cup	parsley, chopped
1/2	cup	white wine
2	tablespoon	lemon juice
	to taste	salt
	to taste	white pepper

Procedure: • *Melt the butter in a large sauté pan and sauté the scallops until firm but not overcooked. Remove the scallops from the sauté pan and set aside.*

Add the the tomatoes and garlic and sauté for 5 minutes. Add the white wine, lemon juice, parsley and reduce until desired consistency.

Return the sea scallops to the sauce. Heat the scallops and season to taste with salt and white pepper.

Serve the scallops topped with the prepared provencale sauce.
Serves 4

Grilled Boneless Quails and Portobello Mushrooms

4		boneless quail
4	small	portobello mushroom
1/2	cup	olive oil
2	tablespoon	lemon juice
2	tablespoon	garlic, chopped
1	cup	duck stock
1/4	cup	red wine
	to taste	salt
	to taste	black pepper

Procedure:

• *Remove the stems from the portobello mushrooms and combine them with the olive oil, lemon and garlic in a mixing bowl. Marinate for at least 30 minutes.*

Reduce the red wine and duck stock to half the original volume.

Preheat a grill surface and season the quails to taste with salt and black pepper. Place the mushrooms on the grill first and cook for 10 minutes before adding the quails. Remove the quails and mushrooms when the quails are completely cooked.

Serve the quails and mushrooms topped with the reduced duck sauce.

Serves 4

Yellowfin Tuna Salsa

8	ounce	yellowfin tuna, diced fine
1	large	yellow onion, diced fine
2	cup	Italian plum tomato, crushed (with juice)
1/4	cup	tomato puree
2	tablespoon	lemon juice
1	tablespoon	white vinegar
1		jalapeno, diced
1/2	bunch	cilantro, chopped
	to taste	salt
		assorted corn chip

Procedure: ▪ Blend all of the ingredients except the corn chips in a mixing bowl and season to taste with salt.

Chill for at least 1 hour and no longer than 6 hours. Toss periodically. Serve with assorted corn chips.
Serves 10

Homemade Duck Sausage

5	pound	boneless pork roast
6	domestic	duck
5	large	yellow onion
3	bunch	green onion
1	cup	garlic clove
2	bunch	basil
	to taste	salt
	to taste	black pepper
	to taste	cayenne pepper

Procedure: ▪ Debone the ducks and reserve all of the fat and organs. Cut the pork into 1 inch cubes. Peel the yellow onions and coarsely chop. Remove the green onion bottoms and coarsely chop.

Run all of the ingredients through a meat grinder with a medium to large grinding plate. Begin with the meat products and finish with the vegetables and herbs followed by a small piece of bread to clear the remaining ingredients from the grinder.

In a mixing bowl, blend thoroughly and season to taste with salt, black pepper and cayenne pepper. Cook small patties to adjust the seasonings.

Form into 4 ounce patties or stuff into sausage casings.

Grill and serve with your favorite sweet mustard.

Makes approximately 12 pounds of sausage which freezes well.
Serves 10

Roasted Sweet Peppers Stuffed with Jalapeno Cheese

4	medium	red sweet pepper
2	cup	monterey jack cheese, grated
2		jalapeno, diced fine
1	teaspoon	garlic, chopped
1/4	cup	olive oil
1	tablespoon	red wine vinegar

Procedure:

- *Roast the sweet peppers over an open flame until the skin is completely charred. Place the peppers in a brown paper bag for 15 minutes and allow them to cool. Rinse the peppers under cool running water to remove the skins. Remove the stems and seeds trying to keep the peppers whole.*

  Blend the cheese, garlic and jalapeno thoroughly and form into 4 equal portions.

  Preheat an oven to 350°. Stuff each pepper with a portion of the cheese mixture and place in a roasting pan. Top the peppers with olive oil and vinegar. Bake until the cheese is completely melted.

  Let stand for 5 minutes and serve topped with the pan drippings.
  Serves 4

Crawfish Purses

1	10x18 sheet	puff pastry dough (prepared)
2		egg yolk
1	pound	crawfish tail
1/2	cup	cream
1	tablespoon	tomato paste
2	tablespoon	romano cheese, grated
1	teaspoon	garlic, chopped
1	teaspoon	lemon juice
1/4	cup	green onion, chopped
	to taste	salt
	to taste	cayenne pepper
1	portion	meuniere sauce (see page 39)

Procedure: ▣ *Prepare the meuniere sauce.*

Heat the crawfish tails in a sauté pan with the cream, tomato paste, romano cheese, garlic, lemon juice and green onions. Bring to a slow boil and season to taste with salt and cayenne pepper. Let cool to room temperature.

Cut the frozen prepared puff pastry sheet into 6, 5x5 inch squares. Place 3 ounces of the crawfish mixture into the center of the pastry squares. Bring the opposite corners together over the center of the crawfish mixture to form a pyramid. Seal the edges completely down the entire length of each seam.

Smooth the egg yolks with a fork. Using a pastry brush paint the entire surface of the crawfish purses with the eggs. Refrigerate.

Preheat an oven to 375°. Bake the crawfish purses for 15 minutes or until crisp and brown. Serve over prepared meuniere sauce.
Serves 6

Cajun Popcorn

1	pound	crawfish tail
2		egg
1	cup	milk
		white flour
	to taste	salt
	to taste	black pepper
	to taste	cayenne pepper
1	portion	remoulade sauce (see page 40)

Procedure: ▣ *Prepare the remoulade sauce.*

Preheat a deep fryer to 375°. Season the white flour to taste with salt, black pepper and cayenne pepper.

Blend the milk and eggs thoroughly. Dip the crawfish tails in the milk wash and dredge through the seasoned flour. Shake off all of the excess flour.

Fry the crawfish tails for approximately 2 minutes or until crisp and brown. Serve with prepared remoulade sauce.
Serves 4

Goat Cheese Stuffed Roma Tomatoes

8		roma tomato
8	ounce	goat cheese
2	cup	proscuitto, sliced
1/2	cup	spinach, cleaned and chopped
		bread crumb
	to taste	salt
	to taste	white pepper

◉ Pesto Sauce

1/2	cup	olive oil, extra virgin
1/4	cup	pine nut
1	cup	fresh basil
1/4	cup	romano cheese, grated
4	clove	garlic
2	teaspoon	crushed red pepper

Procedures:

◉ Pesto Sauce

One day in advance, prepare the pesto sauce by finely grinding all of the ingredients in a food processor.

◉ Roma Tomatoes

Split the roma tomatoes lengthwise. Season to taste with salt and white pepper.

Chop the sliced proscuitto and place on top of the split tomatoes along with the chopped spinach.

Soften the goat cheese in a microwave until pliable but firm. Pipe a rosette on the top of the split stuffed tomatoes. (If a pastry bag is not available, make the goat cheese into balls in the palm of your hand.)

Preheat an oven to 375°. Sprinkle the stuffed tomatoes with bread crumbs. Place them on an oiled sheet pan and bake for 10 minutes or until the cheese is brown on the edges.

Serve on top of the prepared pesto sauce.

Serves 4

Eggplant and Goat Cheese Roulades

1	large	eggplant
2		egg
1/4	cup	milk
2	ounce	romano cheese, grated
1/2	cup	white flour
1/2	cup	olive oil
	to taste	salt
	to taste	black pepper
2	tablespoon	basil, chopped
1	teaspoon	crushed red pepper
1	tablespoon	garlic, chopped
6	ounce	goat cheese
1	portion	marinara sauce (see page 42)

Procedure:

• *Prepare the marinara sauce.*

Slice the eggplant lengthwise into 4 1/8 inch thick slices. Blend the eggs, milk, salt and black pepper in a shallow pan. Combine the flour and romano cheese.

In a food processor, blend the goat cheese, basil, garlic and crushed red pepper until smooth.

Dip the eggplant into the milk wash and transfer to the flour mixture. Coat both sides of the eggplant thoroughly and shake off all of the excess flour.

In a large sauté pan, heat the olive oil until smoking sligthly. Fry the eggplant until brown and soft. Transfer to a paper towel for 5 minutes to cool.

Divide the cheese mixture into 4 equal portions and spread on one side of each eggplant evenly. Starting with the top (or narrow end) of the eggplant slice, roll tightly into a miniature roll.

When ready to serve, preheat an oven to 375°. Bake the roulades for 7 minutes and serve over prepared marinara sauce.
Serves 4

Salads

Vegetables

As a finalist in the 1989 Florida Governor's Cup Seafood Challenge, I was told by one of the judges that the salad course and the vegetable accompaniment would be judged with great emphasis. These often overlooked courses have great potential. As an accessory to a main course, vegetables and salads offer an opportunity to add that special, extra touch. On their own, salads and vegetables are undeniably healthy, appetizing and simple to prepare. Salads and vegetables are no longer simply the necessary green thing on the plate.

The uniqueness of a salad is derived from the choice of lettuce used. A few varieties include Belgian endive, radicchio, arugula and oak leaf blended with spinach. The more commonly used varieties include romaine, iceberg and leaf lettuce.

Contemporary dressings call for simplicity and lightness. Fresh herbs, citruses, mustards and cheeses may be blended with extra virgin olive oils and vinegars to create piquant vinaigrettes.

I have created unusual and successful salad combinations by blending roasted pine nuts, warm goat cheese, roasted peppers and fried seafoods with lettuce mixtures.

Steamed, roasted, boiled, sautéed, baked ~ there are unlimited preparation methods for a winning vegetable dish. New potatoes, roasted with butter and fresh herbs, may be paired creatively with a starchless entrée. An Italian or Cajun style baked vegetable casserole or Southwestern varietal bean preparation will complement a meal perfectly. Often an Oriental style vegetable blends with and enhances grilled fish or roasted meats.

Vegetables and salads have earned a respected place on our menus.

Caesar Salad

1	head	romaine lettuce
2	cup	French bread, cubed
1/4	cup	butter, melted
2		egg yolk
1	tablespoon	Dijon®mustard
1	teaspoon	anchovy, ground
1	tablespoon	garlic, chopped
1	tablespoon	Worcestershire sauce
1	teaspoon	lemon juice
1/4	cup	red wine vinegar
3/4	cup	olive oil
1	cup	romano cheese, grated
	to taste	black pepper

Procedure:

☐ *Toss the diced French bread with the melted butter and brown in a 400° oven for 5 minutes or until brown and crisp.*

In a mixing bowl, blend the eggs, mustard, garlic, anchovies, lemon juice, Worcestershire sauce and vinegar with a wire whip. Mixing continuously, slowly add the olive oil and season to taste with black pepper.

Cut and wash the romaine lettuce in ice water. Toss the romaine lettuce with the dressing, croutons and grated romano cheese.
Serves 4

Hot Crawfish Salad

☐ *Dijon Vinaigrette*

1		egg yolk
1/4	cup	red wine vinegar
1	teaspoon	salt
3	tablespoon	Dijon®mustard
2	cup	olive oil
1/2		red onion, diced
2		green onion, chopped
1/2	rib	celery, diced
1/2		red sweet pepper, diced
1/2		green bell pepper, diced
	to taste	white pepper

▣ Fried Crawfish Tails

1	pound	crawfish tail
1		egg
1	cup	milk
	to taste	salt
	to taste	cayenne pepper
	to taste	granulated garlic
2	cup	white flour

Procedures:

▣ Dijon Vinaigrette

Place the egg yolk, red wine vinegar, salt and mustard in a blender. On high speed, slowly incorporate the olive oil.

Combine the dressing with the chopped vegetables and season to taste with white pepper.

▣ Fried Crawfish Tails

Mix the egg, seasonings to taste and milk. Blend thoroughly.

Preheat a deep fryer to 350°. Prepare 4 portions of selected mixed greens. Place the crawfish tails in the milk wash and toss with the seasoned flour. Shake off all of the excess flour and deep fry for 3 minutes.

Drain the crawfish of excess grease and serve over mixed greens topped with the Dijon vinaigrette.

Serves 4

Fresh Mozzarella with Tomatoes, Red Onion and Basil

1	pound	mozzarella
2	large	tomato, sliced
1	medium	red onion, sliced
1/2	cup	basil, chopped
1/2	cup	olive oil
1/4	cup	balsamic vinegar
1	tablespoon	garlic, chopped
	to taste	salt
	to taste	black pepper

Procedure: • Slice the mozzarella into 12 1/8 inch thick slices. Arrange the mozzarella, red onion and tomato on 4 salad plates.

In a mixing bowl, combine the olive oil, vinegar, garlic and basil. Blend thoroughly and season to taste with salt and black pepper. Serve over the mozzarella salad.

Serves 4

Marinated Avocado, Onion and Tomato Salad

2		tomato
2		avocado
1		red onion
1	head	romaine lettuce
1/2	cup	olive oil
1/4	cup	canola oil
1/3	cup	red wine vinegar
2	teaspoon	garlic, chopped
1	tablespoon	basil, chopped
1/2	cup	feta cheese, crumbled
	to taste	salt
	to taste	black pepper

Procedure: • In a mixing bowl combine the oils, vinegar, garlic, basil and feta cheese. Season to taste with salt and black pepper.

Peel the avocados, remove the seed and cut into cubes. Julienne the red onion and dice the tomato. Place all of these ingredients in the marinade. Let stand for 2 hours, tossing periodically.

Clean and cut the romaine lettuce. Toss the marinated mixture with the romaine lettuce and serve with additional marinade.

Serves 4

Radicchio and Romaine with Hot Proscuitto Vinaigrette

1	head	radicchio
1/2	head	romaine lettuce
4	strip	bacon, fried
1/4	cup	red wine vinegar
1	bunch	green onion, chopped

1	tablespoon	sugar
1/2	cup	olive oil
	to taste	salt
	to taste	black pepper
3/4	cup	romano cheese, grated

Procedure: ● *Clean and cut the radicchio and romaine. Arrange the lettuces on 4 salad plates.*

Crush the fried bacon and combine in a sauté pan with the olive oil, red wine vinegar and sugar. Heat and season to taste with salt and black pepper.

Serve the heated dressing over the lettuces and garnish with the grated romano cheese and chopped green onions.
Serves 4

Mixed California Greens, Asiago Cheese and Balsamic Vinegar

1	head	radicchio
1	bunch	arugula
1	bunch	red oak leaf lettuce
1	bunch	frisée
4	ounce	asiago cheese, shaved (vegetable peeler)
1/3	cup	olive oil
4	tablespoon	balsamic vinegar
1	tablespoon	red wine vinegar
	to taste	salt
	to taste	black pepper

Procedure: ● *Clean and cut the lettuces. Set aside.*

Combine all of the remaining ingredients except the cheese and seasonings in a mixing bowl.

Season to taste with salt and black pepper. Serve garnished with shaved asiago cheese.
Serves 4

Thai Chicken Salad

1		chicken, roasted
1	cup	mushroom, quartered
3/4	cup	canola oil
1/2	cup	soy sauce
1	tablespoon	garlic, chopped
1	teaspoon	ginger, chopped
	to taste	Thai chili sauce (Túóng Ót Tói Viet-nam)
1/4	cup	pineapple juice
1/2	cup	white vinegar
1	teaspoon	sesame oil
1	tablespoon	sugar
1	tablespoon	mint, chopped
1	bunch	green onion, chopped
1/2	head	Napa cabbage, shredded
1	cup	red cabagge, shredded
1	pint	alfalfa sprout
1		gold pepper, julienned

Procedure:

- *Remove the skin and bones from the roasted chicken. Tear the meat into thin strips and chill.*

  Sauté the mushrooms in the canola oil until soft. Add the soy sauce, garlic, ginger, chili sauce, pineapple juice, vinegar, sesame oil, sugar, mint and green onions. Cook an additional 5 minutes, add the chicken and allow to cool.

  Blend the Napa cabbage, red cabbage and gold pepper in a mixing bowl and toss with the chilled marinated chicken and mushrooms.

  Garnish each salad with alfalfa sprouts. Serve with additional marinade as dressing.
  Serves 6

Napa Salad

1	head	radicchio
1/2	head	romaine lettuce, cleaned and cut
1	cup	calamata olive
1/2	cup	sundried tomato
1/2	pound	goat cheese
1/2	cup	olive oil
2	tablespoon	balsamic vinegar
2	tablespoon	red wine vinegar
1/2		red onion, diced fine
1	tablespoon	garlic, chopped
2	tablespoon	basil, chopped
	to taste	salt
	to taste	black pepper

Procedure: ▪ *Blend the olive oil, vinegars, onion, garlic, basil and seasonings in a mixing bowl and chill.*

Form a semi-circular bowl on one side of a salad plate from the curled outer leaves of the radicchio. Place the cut and cleaned romaine lettuce in the center of the bowl. Julienne the sundried tomatoes and place them on top of the romaine lettuce.

Remove the seeds from the olives and split. Slice the goat cheese into 8 equal slices. Top each salad with 2 slices of the goat cheese, olives and basil vinaigrette.
Serves 4

Maytag Bleu Cheese Dressing

1	pound	Maytag bleu cheese, crumbled
3	cup	olive oil
2	tablespoon	garlic, chopped
1/4	cup	basil, chopped
1	cup	red wine vinegar
	to taste	salt
	to taste	black pepper

Procedure: ▪ *Blend all of the ingredients in a mixing bowl and chill. Serve over your favorite selection of mixed greens.*

Hot and Sour Crispy Pork Salad

1/2	pound	pork tenderloin
2		egg white
1	cup	canola oil
1	teaspoon	salt
1	teaspoon	white pepper
1	tablespoon	corn starch
		white flour
1/3	cup	pineapple juice
1/4	cup	red wine vinegar
1/3	cup	ketchup
1	tablespoon	garlic, chopped
1	teaspoon	ginger, chopped
	to taste	crushed red pepper
	pinch	cinnamon
1/2	head	romaine lettuce
2	cup	arugula or spinach
1		sweet red pepper, diced coarse

Procedure:

• Pound the pork tenderloin into thin medallions and cut into julienne strips.

Combine the pork strips with the egg, 3 tablespoons of the canola oil, corn starch, salt and pepper. Blend thoroughly and let stand for 30 minutes.

Combine the pineapple juice, vinegar, ketchup, remaining canola oil, garlic, ginger and cinnamon in a mixing bowl and blend thoroughly. Season to taste with crushed red pepper.

Preheat a deep fryer to 350°. Toss the pork in the white flour, coating thoroughly. Shake off all of the excess flour.

Fry the pork for 3 minutes and transfer to a paper towel to absorb the excess grease. Let stand.

Clean and cut the lettuces. Place the lettuce mixture and sweet peppers in a mixing bowl. Fry the pork for a second time, 3 minutes or until crispy. Add the pork to the mixing bowl. Serve the salad mixture tossed with the hot and sour dressing.
Serves 4

Greek Salad

1/2	head	romaine lettuce
1/2	head	iceberg lettuce
2		tomato, diced
1		cucumber, diced
1	large	yellow onion, julienned
1	cup	calamata olive, pitted and split
1	cup	feta cheese, crumbled
1	pint	alfalfa sprout
1	cup	olive oil
1/2	cup	white vinegar
2	teaspoon	garlic, chopped
1	tablespoon	lemon juice
	to taste	salt
	to taste	black pepper

Procedure:

• *Combine the onions, cucumbers, olives, feta cheese, olive oil, vinegar, garlic, lemon juice, salt and black pepper in a mixing bowl. Marinate for 2 hours tossing periodically.*

Clean and cut the lettuces. Toss the marinated mixture with the lettuces and tomatoes. Serve garnished with the alfalfa sprouts and additional feta cheese.
Serves 6

Sliced Tomatoes and Vidalia Onion with Creole Vinaigrette

2		tomato, sliced
1	large	vidalia onion, sliced
1/2	cup	tomato puree
1/4	cup	Italian plum tomato, crushed
2	teaspoon	horseradish
1	teaspoon	Worcestershire sauce
1	teaspoon	garlic, chopped
1/2	cup	red wine vinegar
1/4	cup	olive oil
2	tablespoon	paprika
	to taste	salt
	to taste	cayenne pepper

Procedure: • Place 3 tomato slices and 2 onion slices on each salad plate.

Combine all of the remaining ingredients except seasonings in a blender and puree. Season to taste with salt and cayenne pepper. Serve over the sliced onions and tomato.
Serves 6

Spinach and Radicchio Salad, Pine Nuts, Baked Goat Cheese

1	head	radicchio
3	cup	spinach, cleaned
12	round	French bread crouton
9	ounce	goat cheese
1/2	cup	pine nut, roasted

• *Basil Vinaigrette*

1/2	cup	olive oil
2	tablespoon	balsamic vinegar
2	tablespoon	red wine vineger
1	tablespoon	garlic, chopped
1	tablespoon	red onion, chopped
1/4	cup	basil, chopped
	to taste	salt
	to taste	black pepper

Procedures: • *Basil Vinaigrette*
Blend all of the ingredients in a mixing bowl and season to taste with salt and black pepper. Chill.

• *Salad*
Preheat an oven to 375˚.

Soften the goat cheese in a microwave and transfer to a pastry bag.

Pipe the goat cheese rosettes on top of the croutons and bake in the oven until brown on the edges.

Clean and cut the spinach and radicchio. Place the lettuces in a mixing bowl with the roasted pine nuts.

Toss the salad mixture with the basil vinaigrette and serve with the baked goat cheese croutons.
Serves 4

Arugula, Radicchio, Roasted Peppers and Bleu Cheese

1	head	radicchio
4	bunch	arugula
3		red sweet pepper, roasted (see method page 24)
1	cup	Maytag bleu cheese, crumbled
1	portion	basil vinaigrette (see page 69)
	to taste	black pepper

Procedure: • *Prepare the basil vinaigrette and roasted peppers, combine and chill.*

Clean and cut the arugula and radicchio. Toss with the vinaigrette, bleu cheese, peppers and season to taste with black pepper.
Serves 4

Thai Vegetable Slaw

1/2	head	Napa cabbage, shredded
1	bunch	green onion, julienned
2	large	carrot, julienned
1	teaspoon	ginger, chopped
1	tablespoon	garlic, chopped
1/2	cup	rice vinegar
1/4	cup	canola oil
1/3	cup	soy sauce
	to taste	Thai chili sauce (Túóng Ót Tói Viet-nam)

Procedure: • *Blend all of the ingredients in a mixing bowl and chill. Season to taste with the Thai chili sauce.*
Serves 6

Steamed Asparagus with Sauce Choron

1	pound	asparagus
1	gallon	water
2	tablespoon	baking soda
1	portion	hollandaise sauce (see page 39)
1	teaspoon	tarragon leaf
1	teaspoon	garlic, chopped
1	tablespoon	tomato paste
	to taste	salt
	to taste	black pepper

Procedure:

• *Prepare the hollandaise sauce and blend in the tarragon, garlic and tomato paste. Season the choron sauce to taste with salt and black pepper.*

Cut a 2 inch segment off the bottom of each asparagus. Bring the water to a boil and add the baking soda and asparagus. Cook for 4 minutes or until the skins are soft but the centers firm.

Transfer the asparagus to ice water to stop the cooking process or serve immediately with the prepared choron sauce.
Serves 6

Glazed Carrots

4	large	carrot
3	cup	water
1/2	stick	butter
3	tablespoon	sugar
	to taste	salt
	to taste	white pepper

Procedure:

• *Peel the carrots and cut into 2 inch segments. Turn the carrots with a paring knife to form a football shape.*

Bring the water to a boil. Add the sugar, butter and carrots. Cook until all of the water has evaporated.

Sauté the carrots until the sugar and butter form a glaze. Season to taste with salt and white pepper.
Serves 4

Caramelized Onions

4	large	yellow onion, julienned
1/2	stick	butter
1	tablespoon	sugar
	to taste	salt
	to taste	black pepper

Procedure: ⊡ *Melt the butter in a large sauté pan. Add the onions and sugar. Sauté, stirring continuously, until the onions are brown. Season to taste with salt and black pepper.*

Serves 4

Grilled Marinated Portobello Mushrooms

4	medium	portobello mushroom
2	cup	olive oil
1/4	cup	lemon juice
1	tablespoon	garlic, chopped
1	tablespoon	basil, chopped
	to taste	salt
	to taste	black pepper

Procedure: ⊡ *Remove the stems from the mushrooms and discard. Clean the mushrooms thoroughly.*

Marinate the mushrooms in the remaining ingredients for 3 hours.

Preheat a grill surface for at least 15 minutes. Grill the mushrooms for 15 minutes or until very soft. Serve with the remaining marinade as a sauce.

Serves 4

Olive Oil

Chilled Thai Marinated Cucumbers

2		cucumber
1	cup	rice vinegar
1	teaspoon	ginger, chopped
1	teaspoon	garlic, chopped
1	tablespoon	cilantro, chopped
2	tablespoon	sugar
2	teaspoon	sesame oil
	to taste	Thai pepper, chopped

Procedure: • *Slice the cucumbers paper thin. Place in a bowl with all of the remaining ingredients. Season to taste with the Thai peppers.*

Marinate for 2 hours tossing periodically. Refrigerate.
Serves 4

Eggplant and Shrimp Casserole

3	large	eggplant
1	tablespoon	salt
1/2	stick	butter
1/2	pound	ground beef
1	large	yellow onion, diced
2	rib	celery, diced
1	tablespoon	garlic, chopped
1/2	pound	baby shrimp
2	cube	chicken bouillon
5	cup	bread crumb
1/4	cup	parsley, chopped
2	shot	Tabasco®
1	cup	romano cheese, grated
	to taste	salt
	to taste	black pepper
	to taste	cayenne pepper

Procedure: • *Peel and dice the eggplants. Place them in boiling water with the tablespoon of salt and cook for 10 minutes. Strain and set aside.*

Melt the butter in a large sauté pan and brown the ground beef. Add the onions, celery and garlic. Sauté for 7 minutes.

Add the shrimp, chicken boullion and sauté until the shrimp are cooked. Add the eggplant, Tabasco®and season to taste with salt, black pepper and cayenne pepper. Simmer for 15 minutes.

Add the bread crumbs, parsley and romano cheese. Transfer to a casserole dish and top with additional bread crumbs and cheese. Bake in a 400° oven for 15 minutes.

Serves 10

Yellow Squash Smothered with Tasso and Shrimp

5	large	yellow squash, sliced
1	stick	butter
1	large	yellow onion, diced
1	tablespoon	garlic, chopped
1	cup	tasso, sliced
1	pound	baby shrimp
2	tablespoon	basil, chopped
1	cup	white wine
1	can	Italian plum tomato, crushed (without juice)
1/2	cup	parsley, chopped
	to taste	salt
	to taste	black pepper

Procedure: • *Melt the butter and sauté the onions and garlic in a large sauté pan for 5 minutes. Add the tasso and cook an additional 5 minutes.*

Add the sliced squash, wine, shrimp, tomato and basil. Cook for 15 minutes.

Season to taste with salt and black pepper and finish with the chopped parsley.

Serves 8

Roasted Potatoes with Rosemary

10		baby red potato
1/4	cup	olive oil
2	tablespoon	rosemary, chopped
	to taste	salt
	to taste	white pepper

Procedure:

• Clean the potatoes and cut into quarters. Toss the potatoes in the olive oil and rosemary and place in a roasting pan.

Bake in a 450° oven for 20 minutes or until brown and cooked throughout.

Season to taste with salt and white pepper.
Serves 4

Celery, Garlic Mashed Potatoes

5		Idaho baking potato
3	rib	celery
1	stick	butter
1	cup	heavy cream
2	tablespoon	garlic, chopped
	to taste	salt
	to taste	black pepper

Procedure:

• Peel the potatoes and cut into 2 inch cubes. Place the potatoes and celery in boiling water until the potatoes are cooked throughout. Transfer the celery to a food processor and puree.

Place the potatoes and celery puree in a mixer and beat until smooth.

Add all of the remaining ingredients and season to taste with salt and black pepper.
Serves 6

Okra and Tomatoes

6	strip	bacon
1	large	yellow onion, diced
2	rib	celery, diced
1/2		bell pepper, diced
1	tablespoon	garlic, chopped
2	pound	okra, sliced
3	can	Italian plum tomato, crushed (with juice)
1	cube	chicken bouillon
1	tablespoon	parsley, chopped
	to taste	salt
	to taste	black pepper
	to taste	cayenne pepper

Procedure:

• *Sauté the bacon strips until brown and crisp. Crush the bacon. Add the onions, celery, bell pepper and garlic. Cook for 10 minutes.*

Add the sliced okra, chicken bouillon, tomatoes and parsley. Cook for 30 minutes stirring continuously. Season to taste with salt, black pepper and cayenne pepper.

Serves 6

Sautéed Escarole

1	head	escarole
1/2	cup	olive oil
2	tablespoon	garlic, chopped
	to taste	salt
	to taste	black pepper

Procedure:

• *Clean and cut the escarole into 1x1 inch pieces.*

Heat the olive oil in a large sauté pan. Add the escarole and garlic. Sauté the escarole for 3 minutes or until completely wilted. Season to taste with salt and black pepper.

Serves 4

Japanese Marinated Eggplant

2		eggplant
1/2	cup	rice vinegar
1/2	cup	soy sauce
1	teaspoon	ginger, chopped
1	tablespoon	garlic, chopped
1	tablespoon	crushed red pepper
1	tablespoon	sugar
1	teaspoon	sesame oil
1		green onion, chopped

Procedure:

• *Cut the top and bottom off the eggplants. Slice the eggplants into 4 inch long,1/2 inch strips.*

Preheat a deep fryer to 375°. Fry the eggplant strips for 1 minute. Toss the eggplant strips with all of the remaining ingredients and marinate for 30 minutes.

Serve hot or cold.
Serves 4

Tuscan Style White Beans

2	cup	white bean
2	quart	water
2	quart	chicken stock
1/4	cup	rosemary, chopped
1/4	cup	olive oil
2	ounce	proscuitto, chopped
	to taste	salt
	to taste	black pepper

Procedure:

• *Place all of the ingredients except seasonings in a pot and bring to a boil.*

Cook for 2 hours or until the beans are soft. Add water if necessary during the cooking process. Season to taste with salt and black pepper.
Serves 4

Grilled Pork Loin Chop, Baby Green Beans, Mashed Potatoes

4	14 ounce	pork loin chop
1/4	cup	butter, melted
		white flour
	to taste	salt
	to taste	white pepper
1/2	cup	white wine
2	cup	veal stock
1/2	cup	butter, melted
1/4	pound	baby green bean (hericot vert)
1	portion	celery, garlic mashed potato (see page 75)
1/2		red sweet pepper, diced fine

Procedure:

Prepare the mashed potatoes and keep warm. Preheat an oven to 400°. Preheat a grill surface.

Clean the pork chops by trimming the excess fat. Season to taste with salt and white pepper. Dust the pork chops with white flour.

Heat a 1/4 cup of butter in a large sauté pan and brown both sides of the pork chops. Transfer to the oven and bake until medium rare, approximately 10 minutes.

Remove the chops from the oven and transfer to the grill to complete the cooking process. Remove the chops and set aside.

In the sauté pan with the pan drippings reduce the white wine and veal stock to half the original volume.

Steam the baby green beans for 3 minutes and sauté in the remaining melted butter. Season to taste with salt and white pepper.

Serve the pork chops with the sautéed baby green beans, mashed potatoes and reduced sauce. Garnish with diced red peppers.

Serves 4

Grilled Norwegian Salmon, Pico de Gallo and Rancheros Sauce

4	7 ounce	salmon filet
1/4	cup	olive oil
	to taste	salt
	to taste	white pepper
1	portion	pico de gallo (see page 30)

Rancheros Sauce

1	cup	veal stock
1/2	cup	tomato puree
1	tablespoon	Worcestershire sauce
2	tablespoon	chili powder
1	teaspoon	garlic, chopped
1/2		yellow onion, diced fine
	to taste	salt
	to taste	cayenne pepper

Cilantro Cream

1/4	cup	sour cream
1	teaspoon	lime juice
1/2	bunch	cilantro
	to taste	salt

Procedures:

Rancheros Sauce
Bring all of the ingredients to a slow boil for 20 minutes and season to taste with salt and cayenne pepper.

Cilantro Cream
Puree all of the ingredients in a food processor and season to taste with salt.

Prepare the pico de gallo.

Norwegian Salmon
Preheat a grill surface.

Brush the salmon filets with olive oil and season to taste with salt and white pepper. Grill the salmon to the desired doneness. Place the rancheros sauce on the base of 4 dinner plates. Place the salmon filet on top of the sauce. Garnish the salmon with prepared pico de gallo. Drizzle the cilantro cream through a squeeze bottle onto the rancheros sauce.

Serves 4

Assorted Grilled Vegetables

1		zucchini, split
1		yellow squash, split
4		asparagus spear, steamed
2		portobello mushroom
4		domestic mushroom
2	head	garlic
2		roma tomato, split
1		gold sweet pepper, quartered
1		red sweet pepper, quartered
1		red onion, sliced
2		baby eggplant, fanned
2		Belgian endive, split
1	ear	corn
4		green onion
		olive oil
	to taste	salt
	to taste	black pepper

Procedure:

• Preheat a grill surface.

Brush all of the vegetables with olive oil and season to taste with salt and black pepper. Wrap the corn and garlic in aluminum foil and grill for 25 minutes.

Remove the foil from the corn and garlic and return to the grill. Add the remaining vegetables to the grill.

Grill until all of the vegetables are cooked, removing each item as it is finished.

Serve hot or cold.

Serves 4

Grilled Jumbo Shrimp, Braised Belgian Endive, Tomato Oil

20	jumbo	shrimp
2	head	Belgian endive
3/4	cup	olive oil
	to taste	salt
	to taste	black pepper
1/4	cup	tomato puree
1	teaspoon	lemon juice
1	tablespoon	garlic, chopped
1	tablespoon	basil, chopped
	to taste	cayenne pepper
1/4	cup	chive, chopped
1/2		sweet red pepper, diced fine

Procedure:

• *Preheat a grill surface.*

Blend a 1/4 cup of olive oil in a food processor with the lemon juice, tomato puree, basil, garlic, salt and cayenne pepper.

Peel the shrimp and brush with olive oil. Season to taste with salt and black pepper.

Cut the base of the endive off so that the leaves can be seperated. Heat a 1/4 cup of olive oil in a sauté pan and quickly braise the endive until wilted slightly. Season to taste with salt and black pepper.

Grill the shrimp until thoroughly cooked and serve over the braised endive with the tomato infused olive oil.

Garnish with the chopped chives and diced sweet peppers.
Serves 4

Black Pepper Crusted Tuna Carpaccio

1/2	pound	yellowfin tuna
		black pepper
1/2	cup	sour cream
1/4	cup	Dijon®mustard
1	teaspoon	garlic powder
2	cup	baby lettuce, assorted
8		chive, whole
1		carrot, shredded

Procedure:

• Roll the outer edges of the tuna steak in the black pepper. Place the tuna steak in a freezer for 30 minutes.

Blend the sour cream, mustard and garlic powder in a mixing bowl. Transfer to a squeeze bottle.

Slice the tuna paper thin on a meat slicer. The tuna meat will be easy to slice frozen.

Arrange the tuna slices on the base of 4 large dinner plates. Blend the greens, chives and shredded carrots.

Drizzle the sauce on the carpaccio with the squeeze bottle and garnish with the assorted greens, carrots and chives.

Serves 4

Black Pepper Crusted Yellowfin Tuna Seared Rare

4	6 ounce	yellowfin tuna steak
		black pepper
1/2	cup	canola oil
4	cup	spinach, cleaned
4	tablespoon	soy sauce
4	tablespoon	rice vinegar
	pinch	ginger, chopped
1	tablespoon	water
2	teaspoon	crushed red pepper
1	tablespoon	chive, chopped
1/2		sweet red pepper, diced
20		chive, whole

Emerald Coast Chef Challenge Grand Award Winner

Procedure:

• Blend the soy sauce, vinegar, ginger, water, crushed red pepper and chopped chives. Let the sauce stand at room temperature for 30 minutes.

Press the black pepper into both sides of the tuna steak.

Heat the canola oil in a sauté pan until very hot. Sear the tuna steaks for 10 seconds on each side and remove from the pan.

Place the spinach in the sauté pan and toss until wilted. Transfer the spinach to 4 large dinner plates.

Thinly slice the tuna across the grain. Arrange the tuna slices over the spinach in a star shape.

Garnish the tuna with diced red pepper, whole chives and finish with the prepared sauce.

Serves 4

Raspberries Denise

1	cup	sugar
1		egg
2		egg white
1/3	cup	canola oil
2	teaspoon	vanilla
3/4	cup	white flour
1/4	cup	almond, ground
4	6 ounce scoop	ice cream, your favorite
1	pint	raspberry
1	pint	blueberry
4	tablespoon	sour cream
2	tablespoon	heavy cream
		mint leaf

Requested by
GOURMET magazine

• Raspberry Coulis

2	pint	raspberry
1	cup	powdered sugar
1/2	cup	water

Procedures:

• Raspberry Coulis

Puree all of the ingredients in a blender. Over a medium fire, bring the coulis to a slow boil for 10 minutes. Remove from the heat and pass through a very fine sieve or chinois. Add additional water if the coulis is too thick. Chill.

• Tulip Cup

Preheat an oven to 350°. In a mixing bowl, combine the sugar, eggs, canola oil, flour, vanilla and almonds. Ladle 2 ounces of the mixture into the center of a greased cookie sheet. Form a 7 inch circle.

Bake until the edges are brown. Remove the shell from the cookie sheet quickly with a metal spatula. Transfer the shell to an inverted glass tumbler and gently mold the shell around the base of the glass to form a tulip shape. Allow to cool completely.

Place the raspberry coulis on the base of 4 platters. Combine the cream and sour cream in a squeeze bottle and decorate the coulis. Drag a tooth pick through the white sauce to make the designs. Place the ice cream in the tulip cup with the berries and garnish with fresh mint leaves. Place this assembly on top of the sauce decoration.

Serves 4

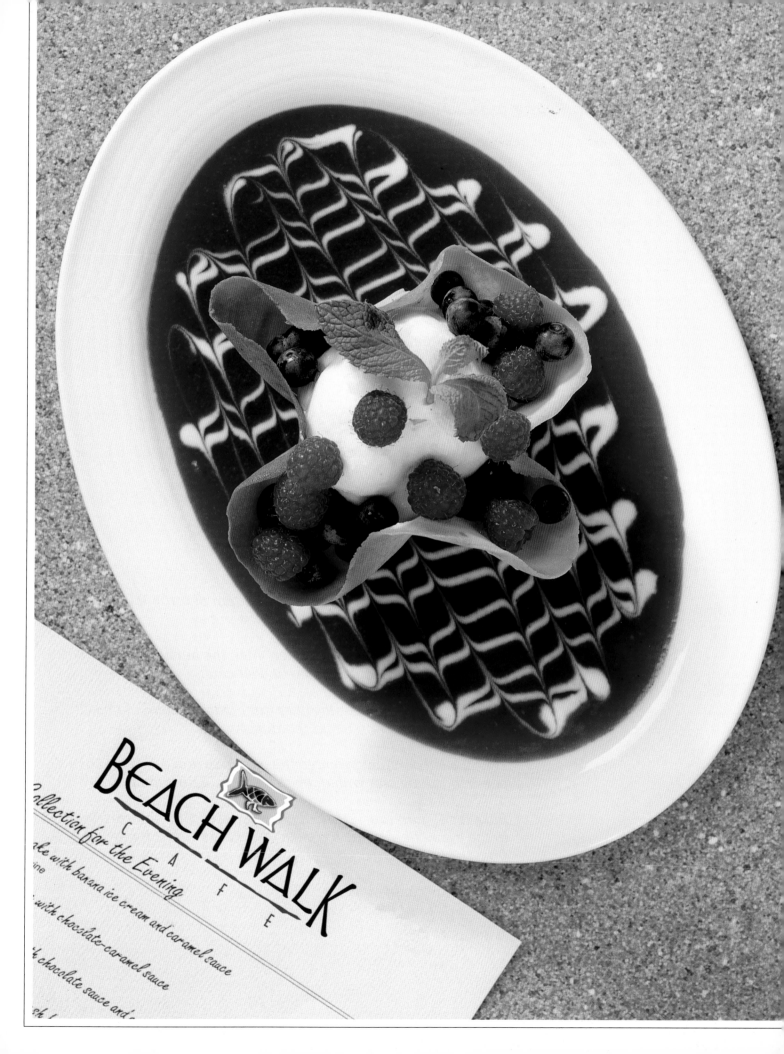

BEACH WALK
C   A   F   F   E

...llection for the Evening

...ke with banana ice cream and caramel sauce
...ine

... with chocolate-caramel sauce

...h chocolate sauce and'

Chocolate Sin Cake with Espresso Cream

15	ounce	semi-sweet chocolate
15	ounce	unsalted butter
2	cup	sugar
12	large	egg
1/2	portion	raspberry coulis (see page 90)
		mint leaf

• Espresso Cream

3	cup	heavy cream
1	cup	sugar
2	tablespoon	espresso, ground

• Chocolate Sauce

4	ounce	semi-sweet chocolate
3/4	cup	heavy cream

• Mango Sauce

2		mango, peeled and seeded
1/4	cup	sugar
2	tablespoon	heavy cream

Procedures:

• Chocolate Sin Cake

Preheat an oven to 350°. Butter the bottom of a 10 inch round cake pan and line the bottom with wax paper.

Combine the chocolate and butter. Melt the butter and chocolate completely over a double boiler and let cool.

Whip the eggs and sugar together until foamy. Combine the 2 mixtures together and blend thoroughly.

Pour the sin cake mixture into the cake pan and place the cake pan in a baking pan with at least 1 1/2 inches of water.

Bake for 45 minutes. Turn off the oven and allow the cake to cool in the oven. Refrigerate the cake for 2 hours before removing from the pan.

Prepare the coulis sauce.

- *Espresso Cream*
  Blend the heavy cream and sugar in a mixing bowl and whip until stiff peaks form. Fold in the espresso grounds.

- *Chocolate Sauce*
  Combine the chocolate and cream in a mixing bowl and melt over a double boiler stirring continuously. Allow to cool to room temperature.

- *Mango Sauce*
  Puree the mangos, sugar and cream in a food processor until smooth. Chill.

Place the 3 sauces in squeeze bottles. Decorate the base of 12 dessert plates.

Slice the sin cake into 12 equal slices and place in the center of the plates.

Place the espresso cream in a pastry bag with a star tip. Pipe the cream on the top of each slice and garnish with fresh mint.

Serves 12

BEACH WALK
CAFE

It is my belief that the most enjoyment of wine comes from tasting a variety of different types and styles. There will always be new wines to taste and new combinations of wine with food to try. Taste a different wine every day of your life and you will only scratch the surface of what there is to learn.

Therefore, my wine suggestions for each dish will be governed by only one rule; variety is the spice of life!

Some classic pairings are simply hard to beat.

They are the result of years of trial and sometimes error. Some wines seem to have a natural affinity for certain foods. An outstanding Montrachet has that affinity for a fine piece of salmon. Of course a mature chardonnay from California, Australia or Spain will give you paralleled results at a fraction of the cost.

Pork will show off many wines well. Try a full-bodied chardonnay or a lighter bodied red such as Beaujolais or a pinot noir.

The best match for vegetables would be wines with a bit of residual sugar. When you think of sweet wines, those from the German Mosel or Rheingau regions are the first that come to mind. A gewurztraminer from Sonoma county is also a fine companion.

Muscadet and Chablis are good choices for shellfish. Chef Tim, however, does like to make your choice interesting by putting a pungent ingredient like Belgian endive in this dish. Rather than competing with the intense flavor, complement it with a semi-sweet styled Vouvray or chenin blanc.

Black pepper crusted tuna calls for an adventurous combination of red wine with fish. A Côtes du Rhone or other red from the northern Rhone region of France with a slight chill has just the right amount of spice to enhance this dish.

There are some dessert wines that are better than others. The finest are from the Sauternes and Barsac region of France. Auslese and sweeter styles from Germany as well as late harvested varieties from California such as Johannisberg riesling and gewurztraminer make a happy partner with the Raspberries Denise.

Choosing a wine to go along with chocolate is difficult. The sweetest, richest wine you can find such as porto or a similar styled Australian wine is best. However, I've found that a fine brandy from Cognac or Armagnac actually complements a dessert as rich and dense as the Chocolate Sin Cake, as well as any wine.

As was said earlier, variety in food and wine pairings is what we find most rewarding, but if there is one rule of thumb it is to drink wines that you enjoy with the meal you're having and there's no way you'll be disappointed. Remember, the more you experiment, the more you'll learn.

Ted Straub, Sommelier, 1987 Best of Show Award Winner at the Atlanta International Wine Festival

Pastas
Grains

Pasta is available in numerous shapes, sizes and applications. A less explored, but equally pleasant counterpart may be found with polenta, a grain product. Polenta has been a part of Italian cuisine for hundreds of years and is only recently being utilized in America's restaurants. This cornmeal product can be served as a hot side dish, formed into cakes and grilled or lightly sweetened as the base for an exciting dessert.

Risotto, an Italian rice product, is available in four lengths. Super fino (extra long) or fino (long) are preferred for preparing this delicate rice dish. The precise, but simple, cooking technique yields a creamy, al dente rice dish. Risotto is complemented by the addition of a choice of meat, seafood, vegetable or herb combination blended in during the cooking process.

Final pasta preparation may be simplified by cooking dry pastas al dente in advance and then chilling and tossing with olive oil.

I use only high quality, imported pastas for menu items. I do not recommend the use of homemade or fresh pasta. The lack of semolina flour or the use of high-pressure extrusion pasta makers result in a limp, gummy pasta product. Cooking time is so critical that thirty seconds will often make or break the quality of the pasta's texture. These pasta have little form and are high in starch content.

The sauce recipes in this section are full of zip. A sauce's flavor in the pot is greatly reduced when almost tasteless pasta is added. Therefore, I recommend over-seasoning your sauces. Italian sauces are but one of many styles of sauces to be used with pastas. Cajun style fettuccine with sautéed baby shrimp, andouille sausage, crawfish tails and a tomato cream sauce showcase a Louisiana flair.

Once you have tried a few of the risotto and polenta dishes, I know you will fall in love with their unique texture and essence. Close attention to the details of preparing these two items will insure success.

The pasta recipes following will require the use of a good quality imported dry pasta to obtain the al denté texture which is authentic to Italian pasta preparations. The recipes will call for cooked and chilled pasta. This method involves bringing water to a rapid boil and cooking the pasta to a point where the outer surface of the pasta is soft but the center is still firm. Removing the pasta and immediately immersing the pasta in ice water to stop the cooking process. The pasta can then be tossed with a small amount of olive oil to keep it from sticking together. This product can be used for up to eight hours after being prepared.

Linguini Pomodoro

1/2	pound	linguini, cooked and chilled
1/2	cup	olive oil
2	cup	Italian plum tomato, crushed
1	tablespoon	garlic, chopped
3	tablespoon	basil, chopped
	to taste	black pepper
		romano cheese, grated

Procedure:

• *Heat the olive oil in a large sauté pan. Add the tomatoes and garlic and sauté for 2 minutes.*

Add the basil and black pepper to taste. Add the pasta and toss until the pasta is heated thoroughly.

Serve with grated romano cheese.
Serves 4

Fettuccine Carbonara

1/2	pound	fettuccine, cooked and chilled
3	ounce	proscuitto, sliced and julienned
3	cup	heavy cream
2		egg yolk
1	tablespoon	garlic, chopped
1	cup	romano cheese, grated
	to taste	black pepper

Procedure:

• In a large sauté pan fry the proscuitto for 3 minutes.

Whip the egg and cream together. Add the garlic to the fried proscuitto and sauté. Do not brown. Add the cream and egg mixture stirring continuously. Bring to a slow boil.

Add the romano cheese and black pepper and return to a slow boil. Add the pasta and toss until the pasta is heated thoroughly.

Serve with grated romano cheese.
Serves 4

Cajun Fettuccine

1/2	pound	fettuccine, cooked and chilled
1/4	cup	butter, melted
1/4	pound	andouille sausage, julienned
1	tablespoon	garlic, chopped
1	cup	mushroom, sliced
1/4	cup	green onion, chopped
1/4	pound	baby shrimp
1/4	pound	crawfish tail
1/3	cup	white wine
1/4	cup	lemon juice
2	tablespoon	tomato paste
1	cup	heavy cream
3/4	cup	grated romano cheese
	to taste	salt
	to taste	white pepper

Requested by GOURMET magazine

Procedure:

• In a large sauté pan, heat the butter and sauté the andouille sausage, green onions, garlic, mushrooms, crawfish and shrimp for 3 minutes.

Blend the heavy cream and tomato paste thoroughly.

Add the white wine, lemon juice and cream mixture to the sauté pan and reduce for 3 minutes. Add the romano cheese and season to taste with salt and white pepper. Add the pasta and toss until the pasta is heated thoroughly.

Serve with grated romano cheese.
Serves 4

Penne Amatriciana

1⁄2	pound	penne, cooked and chilled
1⁄2	cup	olive oil
2	cup	Italian plum tomato, crushed
1	tablespoon	garlic, chopped
3	tablespoon	basil, chopped
1	ounce	proscuitto, sliced and julienned
	to taste	crushed red pepper
		romano cheese, grated

Procedure:

• *Heat the olive oil in a large sauté pan. Add the proscuitto, tomatoes and garlic, sauté for 3 minutes.*

Add the basil and crushed red pepper to taste. Add the pasta and toss until the pasta is heated thoroughly.

Serve with grated romano cheese.
Serves 4

Rigatoni with Roasted Chicken and Sweet Peppers

1⁄2	pound	rigatoni, cooked and chilled
3⁄4	cup	olive oil
1		chicken, roasted
1	tablespoon	garlic, chopped
1⁄2		red sweet pepper, julienned
1⁄2		gold sweet pepper, julienned
3	tablespoon	basil, chopped
	to taste	salt
	to taste	crushed red pepper
		romano cheese, grated

Procedure:

• *Remove the skin from the chicken and debone the meat. Cut the meat into julienne strips.*

Heat the olive oil in a large sauté pan. Add the peppers, basil, garlic, chicken, salt and red pepper to taste. Sauté for 2 minutes.

Add the pasta and toss until the pasta is heated thoroughly.

Serve with grated romano cheese.
Serves 4

Bowtie Pasta, Broccoli, Fontina Cream, Crispy Proscuitto

1/2	pound	bowtie pasta, cooked and chilled
2	cup	heavy cream
1	cup	fontina cheese, grated
2	cup	broccoli floret, steamed
1	tablespoon	garlic, chopped
4	ounce	proscuitto, sliced and julienned
	to taste	black pepper
		romano cheese, grated

Procedure:

• *Preheat a deep fryer to 350°. Fry the julienned proscuitto until crispy. Set aside.*

Heat the cream in a large sauté pan and add the fontina cheese, garlic and black pepper to taste. Bring to a slow boil.

Add the steamed broccoli and pasta. Toss until the pasta is heated thoroughly.

Serve the pasta topped with the crispy proscuitto and grated romano cheese.

Serves 4

Bowtie Pasta, Spinach and Roasted Duck

1/2	pound	bowtie pasta, cooked and chilled
1		duck, roasted
1/4	cup	duck oil (reserved from roasted duck)
2	tablespoon	garlic, chopped
2	cup	spinach, cleaned
	to taste	crushed red pepper
3/4	cup	duck stock
2	tablespoon	soy sauce
		romano cheese, grated

Procedure:

• *Remove the skin from the duck and debone the meat. Cut the meat into julienne strips.*

Heat the duck oil in a large sauté pan. Add the duck meat, garlic, red pepper and sauté for 4 minutes. Add the duck stock and soy sauce and bring to a slow boil.

Add the spinach and pasta. Toss until the pasta is heated thoroughly.

Serve topped with the grated romano cheese.
Serves 4

Rigatoni with Four Cheeses and Roma Tomatoes

1/2	pound	rigatoni, cooked and chilled
1/3	cup	bel paesa cheese, grated
1/3	cup	fontina cheese, grated
1/3	cup	romano cheese, grated
2	cup	heavy cream
	to taste	black pepper
1/4	cup	basil, chopped
3		roma tomato, diced
1	cup	asiago cheese, shaved

Procedure: • *Heat the cream in a large sauté pan. Add the bel paesa, fontina and romano cheeses.*

Cook until all of the cheeses are completely melted.

Season to taste with black pepper. Add the pasta and toss until the pasta is heated thoroughly.

Serve the pasta garnished with chopped basil, diced roma tomatoes and shaved asiago cheese.
Serves 4

Linguini with Grilled Italian Sausage and Zucchini

1/2	pound	linguini, cooked and chilled
2	pound	Italian sausage
2		zucchini
3	tablespoon	olive oil
	to taste	salt
	to taste	white pepper
2	portion	marinara sauce (see page 42)
		romano cheese, grated

Procedure:

• *Prepare the marinara sauce.*

Preheat a grill surface. Split the zucchini lengthwise and brush with olive oil. Season to taste with salt and white pepper.

Grill the Italian sausage and zucchini. Keep hot. Heat half of the marinara sauce in a large sauté pan. Add the pasta and toss until the pasta is heated thoroughly.

Cut the zucchini and Italian sausage into 1 inch segments. Serve on top of the pasta with grated romano cheese and additional marinara sauce.

Serves 4

Penne Puttanesca

1/2	pound	penne, cooked and chilled
1/2	cup	olive oil
2	cup	Italian plum tomato, crushed
1	tablespoon	garlic, chopped
1	tablespoon	caper
1/4	cup	calamata olive, pitted and split
1/4	cup	basil, chopped
	to taste	crushed red pepper
		romano cheese, grated

Procedure:

• *Heat the olive oil in a large sauté pan. Add the olives, capers, tomatoes and garlic, sauté for 3 minutes.*

Add the basil and crushed red pepper to taste.

*Add the pasta and toss until the pasta is heated thoroughly.
Serve with grated romano cheese.*
Serves 4

Linguini with Tomato and Pecan Pesto Sauce

1/2	pound	linguini, cooked and chilled
1/4	cup	olive oil
2	portion	pesto sauce (see page 56)
1/4	cup	pecan, finely chopped
3/4	cup	Italian plum tomato, crushed
	to taste	crushed red pepper
		romano cheese, grated

Procedure: ▣ *Prepare the pesto sauce.*

Heat the pesto sauce and olive oil in a large sauté pan. Add the pecans, tomatoes and red pepper to taste. Sauté for 5 minutes.

Add the pasta and toss until the pasta is heated thoroughly.

Serve with grated romano cheese.
Serves 4

Bowtie Pasta with Uncooked Tomato Sauce

1/2	pound	bowtie pasta, cooked and chilled
3		tomato
1/4	cup	olive oil
4		garlic clove, sliced
1/4	cup	basil, chopped
	to taste	salt
	to taste	crushed red pepper
		romano cheese, grated

Procedure: • *Bring a pot of water to a boil. Cut an "X" in the skin on the bottom of each tomato. Place the tomatoes in the boiling water for 3 minutes.*

Transfer the tomatoes to ice water to stop the cooking process. Peel the skins off the tomatoes by placing the blade of a paring knife under the skin where it has been freed by the "X" cut.

Cut off the tops of the tomatoes and dice fine.

Heat the olive oil in a large sauté pan. Sauté the garlic and basil for 2 minutes. Add the pasta and tomatoes. Toss until the pasta and tomatoes are heated thoroughly.

Season to taste with salt and crushed red pepper. Serve with grated romano cheese.
Serves 4

Rigatoni Aglio & Olio

1/2	pound	rigatoni, cooked and chilled
1/2	cup	olive oil
2	tablespoon	garlic, chopped
2	tablespoon	basil, chopped
1	teaspoon	lemon juice
	to taste	salt
	to taste	crushed red pepper
		romano cheese, grated

Procedure: • *Heat the olive oil in a large sauté pan. Add the garlic and fry until slightly brown. Transfer the garlic to a paper towel to dry.*

Add the lemon juice, basil and pasta to the sauté pan and toss until the pasta is heated thoroughly.

Season to taste with salt and red pepper. Serve topped with the fried garlic and grated romano cheese.
Serves 4

Fettuccine with Crawfish Tails and Tasso Cream Sauce

1/2	pound	fettuccine, cooked and chilled
1/4	pound	tasso, shaved
3	cup	heavy cream
1	cup	romano cheese, grated
1	pound	crawfish tail
1	bunch	green onion, chopped

Procedure:

• *Heat the cream and tasso in a large sauté pan. Add the crawfish tails and romano cheese. Bring the sauce to a boil and reduce for 3 minutes.*

Add the pasta and toss until the pasta is heated thoroughly.

Serve the pasta garnished with chopped green onions and grated romano cheese.

Serves 4

Penne with Italian Sausage, Spinach and Fontina Cheese

1/2	pound	penne, cooked and chilled
1/4	cup	olive oil
1	tablespoon	garlic, chopped
2	pound	Italian sausage
2	cup	Italian plum tomato, crushed
2	cup	spinach, cleaned
1	cup	fontina cheese, grated
	to taste	crushed red pepper

Procedure:

• *Heat the olive oil in a large sauté pan. Cut the Italian sausage into 1 inch segments and sauté with the garlic in the olive oil for 5 minutes.*

Add the tomatoes and crushed red pepper to taste. Add the pasta and spinach. Toss until the pasta is heated thoroughly.

Serve garnished with grated fontina cheese.

Serves 4

Rigatoni, Portobello Mushrooms, Chicken and Spicy Spinach Oil

1/2	pound	rigatoni, cooked and chilled
2	cup	spinach, cleaned
1	cup	olive oil
1	tablespoon	crushed red pepper
1		chicken, roasted
2	large	portobello mushroom, sliced
	to taste	salt
		romano cheese, grated

Procedure:

- Place the spinach, olive oil and crushed red pepper in a blender and puree.

Remove the skin from the chicken and debone the meat. Cut the meat into julienne strips.

Heat the spinach oil in a large sauté pan. Add the mushrooms and cook until soft. Add the chicken and season to taste with salt.

Add the pasta and toss until the pasta is heated thoroughly.

Serve topped with grated romano cheese.

Serves 4

Bowtie Pasta, Baby Shrimp, Ginger and Thai Chili Sauce

1/2	pound	bowtie pasta, cooked and chilled
1/4	cup	canola oil
1	tablespoon	garlic, chopped
2	teaspoon	ginger, chopped
3/4	pound	baby shrimp
3	tablespoon	rice vinegar
1/4	cup	soy sauce
	to taste	Thai chili sauce (Túóng Ót Tói Viet-nam)
1	bunch	green onion, chopped

Procedure: • Heat the canola oil in a large sauté pan. Add the garlic, ginger and baby shrimp. Sauté until the shrimp are cooked thoroughly.

Add the rice vinegar, soy sauce and Thai chili sauce to taste. Add the pasta and green onions. Toss until the pasta is heated thoroughly.

Serve with grated romano cheese.

Serves 4

Penne with Sweet Corn Poblano Sauce, Baby Shrimp, Tomato

1/2	pound	penne, cooked and chilled
1	can	corn (with juice)
1		poblano pepper, roasted (see page 42)
1	tablespoon	garlic, chopped
1/2	cup	heavy cream
1/2	pound	baby shrimp
2		tomato, diced
	to taste	salt
		romano cheese, grated

Procedure: • Place the corn, roasted poblano pepper and garlic in a blender and puree.

Heat the cream in a large sauté pan. Add the pureed mixture and bring to a slow boil. Add the shrimp and boil until cooked thoroughly. Season to taste with salt.

Add the pasta and toss until the pasta is heated thoroughly.

Garnish with the diced tomatoes and grated romano cheese.

Serves 4

Spinach and Goat Cheese Stuffed Pasta Shells

16	large	pasta shell, cooked and chilled
9	ounce	goat cheese
3	cup	spinach, cleaned and chopped
	to taste	black pepper
2	portion	marinara sauce (see page 42)
		romano cheese, grated

Procedure: ▪ *Prepare the marinara sauce.*

Place the spinach and goat cheese in a food processor and blend well. Season to taste with black pepper.

Preheat an oven to 350°. Stuff each shell with the goat cheese mixture. Place all of the stuffed shells in a baking pan. Top each shell with 1 ounce of marinara sauce.

Bake for 10 minutes. Remove from the oven and serve with heated marinara sauce and grated romano cheese.
Serves 4

Grated Pasta with Tomato Broth

2		egg
2	cup	white flour
3	tablespoon	canola oil
2	tablespoon	bacon grease
4	tablespoon	tomato paste
7	cup	water
	to taste	salt
	to taste	black pepper

Procedure: ▪ *Blend the eggs and flour together. Knead the dough until smooth, dry texture. Let the dough rest for 15 minutes.*

Using the small side of a cheese grater, grate the dough into small pieces. Let dry.

Bring the water to a boil in a pot. Add the grated dough, bacon grease, oil and tomato paste. Simmer for 20 minutes, stirring periodically. Season to taste with salt and black pepper.
Serves 4

Manicotti Vignone

6		egg
2	cup	milk
1 1/2	cup	white flour

· Filling

2	pound	ricotta cheese
2		egg
1/2	cup	parmesan cheese, grated
2	tablespoon	parsley, chopped

· Meatballs

2	pound	ground beef
2		egg
4	slice	white bread
1/3	cup	romano cheese, grated

· Red Sauce

2	# 10 can	Italian plum tomato
6	ounce	tomato paste
1		yellow onion, diced
6	clove	garlic, crushed
2	pound	Italian sausage, roasted (reserve 2 tablespoons grease)
	to taste	sugar
	to taste	salt
	to taste	black pepper

Procedures:

· Red Sauce

Run the 2 cans of tomatoes with juice through a food mill and discard the pulp. Transfer to a large sauce pot.

Add the tomato paste, garlic, onions and sausage grease. Bring to a slow boil and reduce to a simmer for at least 8 hours. Add the sausage and prepared meat balls. Season to taste with salt, black pepper and sugar. Keep warm.

· Meatballs

Soften the bread with warm water. Blend the ground beef, eggs, bread and cheese together and mix thoroughly. Be certain to break the bread into small pieces while mixing.

Preheat an oven to 375°. Form this mixture into balls and place in a roasting pan. Bake the meatballs for 15 minutes on one side, turn the meatballs over and bake another 15 minutes. Remove and allow to cool.

Filling
Blend all of the ingredients in a mixing bowl. Chill.

Manicotti Shell
Beat the eggs until foamy, blend in the flour with a wire whip. Once the flour has been completely incorporated slowly whip in the milk.

Preheat an electric skillet to 200°. Place 2 tablespoons of the mixture into the skillet and cook until the visible side is dry. Transfer to a paper towel. Repeat this procedure until all of the mixture is used.

Preheat an oven to 350°. Place 2 tablespoons of the ricotta cheese filling on the center of each pasta shell. Fold the 2 opposite edges together. They should meet at the center and overlap somewhat.

In 2 large roasting pans place enough red sauce to cover the base of the pan. Arrange the manicotti side by side in the pan. Top the manicotti with red sauce.

Cover the roasting pans with aluminum foil. Bake the manicotti for 30 minutes. Remove from the oven and let rest for 5 minutes covered.

Remove the manicotti from the roasting pan with a metal spatula and serve with additional red sauce and grated parmesan cheese.

Serves 8

Fried Rice

2	cup	rice
2	tablespoon	hoisin sauce
1/3	cup	canola oil
3		egg, whipped
2	teaspoon	garlic, chopped
1	teaspoon	ginger, chopped
1/2	cup	onion, diced fine
1	cup	green pea
1	cup	carrot, diced fine
1/4	cup	oyster sauce
2	tablespoon	soy sauce
2	teaspoon	sherry
2	tablespoon	sugar
2	teaspoon	sesame oil
	to taste	black pepper

Procedure:

• Blend the hoisin sauce with the rice and boil or steam the rice. Cook until dry. Cool.

Heat the oil in a wok. Add the garlic, ginger, onions, peas and carrots and sauté for 1 minute.

Add the whipped eggs and cook like an omelet.

Break the egg mixture into pieces and add the rice. Toss all of the remaining sauce ingredients together with the rice. Season to taste with black pepper.

Add additional oil if the rice seems to be sticking. Sauté the rice until heated thoroughly. Serve immediately.

Serves 4

Jambalaya

1	pound	pork roast, diced
1		chicken, roasted, deboned and sliced
1	tablespoon	cayenne pepper
1	tablespoon	granulated garlic
1	6 ounce bottle	Worcestershire sauce
2	large	yellow onion, diced
4	rib	celery, diced
1		bell pepper, diced
2	tablespoon	garlic, chopped
1	can	cream of mushroom soup
3	quart	chicken stock
3	tablespoon	Kitchen Bouquet®
1	pound	smoked sausage, sliced
5	cup	Uncle Ben's® rice
2	cup	green onion, chopped
	to taste	salt
	to taste	black pepper

Procedure:

• In a heavy black iron pot, fry the pork until the water has evaporated and only the oil remains.

Add the Worcestershire sauce, cayenne pepper and granulated garlic. Add the onions, celery, bell pepper and garlic. Sauté for 10 minutes.

Add the remaining ingredients except the rice and seasonings. Bring to a boil. Season to taste with salt and black pepper. (When seasoning, consider the volume of the rice and it will be necessary to over season the liquid mixture.)

Add the rice and boil for 10 minutes. Reduce to a simmer, cover and cook for 45 minutes stirring periodically.

Serve immediately.

Serves 12

Andouille Rice

2	cup	rice, cooked
1/2	pound	andouille sausage, ground fine
1	tablespoon	garlic, chopped
1	cup	green onion, chopped

Procedure: • *In a sauté pan, cook the andouille and garlic for 10 minutes.*

Add the rice and green onions and sauté until the rice is heated thoroughly.
Serves 4

Polenta Marinara

12	ounce	yellow cornmeal
13	cup	water
1	cup	parmesan cheese, grated
	to taste	salt
	to taste	black pepper
1	portion	marinara sauce (see page 42)

Procedure: • *Prepare the marinara sauce. Keep warm.*

Bring the water to a boil and add the cornmeal. Reduce to a simmer and cook for 25 minutes.

Stir in the parmesan cheese and season to taste with salt and black pepper. Add additional water if the polenta is too thick for desired consistency.

Blend a 1/4 of the marinara sauce into the polenta and serve the remaining marinara sauce over the polenta.
Serves 8

Grilled Polenta and Baby Eggplant with Pomodoro Sauce

12	ounce	yellow cornmeal
11	cup	water
1/2	cup	romano cheese, grated
	to taste	salt
	to taste	black pepper
2	tablespoon	butter
16	ounce	goat cheese
8		baby eggplant
		olive oil
1	portion	pomodoro sauce (see page 99)

Procedure:

• Bring the water to a boil and add the cornmeal. Reduce to a simmer and cook for 25 minutes.

Stir in the romano cheese and butter. Season to taste with salt and black pepper.

Pour the polenta mixture onto an oiled sheet pan 1/2 inch deep. Cover and refrigerate for 1 hour.

Prepare the pomodoro sauce and keep warm.

Preheat a grill surface.

Cut the eggplant into fan shapes by making 1/8 inch cuts lengthwise from the top of the eggplant down. Leaving the top 1/2 inch of the eggplant connected.

Brush the eggplant with olive oil and season to taste with salt and black pepper. Cut the chilled polenta into 16 2x2 inch squares.

Place the eggplant and polenta on the grill and cook until the eggplant is soft.

Place 2 polenta cakes on each plate with 1 grilled eggplant. Top each polenta cake with a 2 ounce slice of goat cheese. Place the entire plate under a broiler to heat.

Serve topped with the prepared pomodoro sauce.
Serves 8

Baked Polenta with Grilled Portobello Mushrooms

12	ounce	yellow cornmeal
11	cup	water
	to taste	salt
	to taste	white pepper
4		egg white
1/2	cup	fontina cheese, grated
8	medium	portobello mushroom
1	cup	olive oil
1	tablespoon	garlic, chopped
1/4	cup	lemon juice
1/2	cup	Madeira wine
4	cup	veal stock

Procedure:

• *Clean the portobello mushrooms and remove the stems. Marinate the mushrooms in the olive oil, garlic and lemon juice for 30 minutes.*

Bring the water to a boil and add the cornmeal. Reduce to a simmer and cook for 15 minutes.

Stir in the egg whites and fontina cheese. Season to taste with salt and white pepper.

Preheat an oven to 350°. Pour the polenta mixture into a 8x8 inch cake pan and bake for 20 minutes. Let cool to room temperature.

Reduce the veal stock and Madeira wine by half the original volume. Keep warm.

While the polenta is baking, preheat a grill surface. Grill the portobello mushrooms until soft. Keep warm.

Cut the polenta into 3x3 inch square cakes. Cut the mushrooms into quarters. Place the polenta in the center of the plate and surround with 4 mushroom quarters.

Serve topped with the reduced sauce and garnish with fresh herbs.

Serves 8

Risotto with Asparagus and Crabmeat

8	ounce	arborio rice
3	tablespoon	olive oil
5	cup	chicken stock
1	cup	heavy cream
3⁄4	cup	fontina cheese, grated
1⁄2	pound	asparagus, chopped
1⁄2	pound	lump crabmeat
	to taste	salt
	to taste	black pepper
	to taste	romano cheese, grated

Procedure:

- *In a large sauté pan, heat the olive oil. Add the rice and toss until all of the rice has been coated with oil.*

  Add the chicken stock and bring to a slow boil for 10 minutes, stirring periodically.

  Add the heavy cream and asparagus and slow boil for 5 minutes.

  Add the lump crabmeat, fontina cheese, romano cheese and season to taste with salt and black pepper.

  Cook for an additional 3 to 5 minutes stirring continuously. The rice should be al denté after 18 to 20 minutes total cooking time.

  The rice may be cooked longer to achieve a softer consistency. Simply add more water or chicken stock if the risotto begins to get dry and cook until the desired texture is achieved.

  Serve immediately with grated romano cheese.

  Serves 4

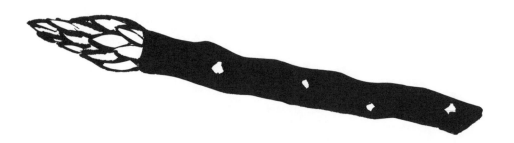

Risotto with Mushrooms, Fontina Cheese and Basil

8	ounce	arborio rice
3	tablespoon	olive oil
5	cup	chicken stock
1	cup	heavy cream
3/4	cup	fontina cheese, grated
2	cup	mushroom, sliced
1/4	cup	basil, chopped
	to taste	salt
	to taste	black pepper
	to taste	romano cheese, grated

Procedure:

In a large sauté pan, heat the olive oil. Add the rice and toss until all of the rice has been coated with oil.

Add the chicken stock and bring to a slow boil for 10 minutes, stirring periodically.

Add the heavy cream and slow boil for an additional 5 minutes.

Add the mushrooms, fontina cheese, romano cheese, basil and season to taste with salt and black pepper.

Cook for an additional 3 to 5 minutes stirring continuously. The rice should be al denté after 18 to 20 minutes total cooking time.

The rice may be cooked longer to achieve a softer consistency. Simply add more water or chicken stock if the risotto begins to get dry and cook until the desired texture is achieved.

Serve immediately with grated romano cheese.
Serves 4

These 2 risotto recipes provide you with a great base to begin creating your own risotto dishes. Remember that the overall cooking time is 18 to 20 minutes and consider this when adding your selected ingredients. The ingredients you choose should be added at a point in the cooking process that will allow them their normal cooking time. Do not add products early because they cannot be removed and the risotto's cooking time cannot be shortened.

MPoultry
eats

Everyone enjoys a prime aged steak charbroiled and sizzling on a hot plate in its own natural juices. Perhaps a domestic rack of lamb with fresh rosemary, garlic and finished with a red wine reduction sauce or a grilled thick cut pork chop, natural juices and celery garlic mashed potatoes. Regardless of the particular type of meat or poultry that you crave most, in this day and age of heart healthiness, when it's time to spoil yourself, it needs to be at its very best.

I am very particular about the grade of beef, lamb, poultry, pork and veal selected to be served in our dining room. Only U.S.D.A. prime beef is purchased, this being the select one percent of all beef graded in the country. Certified Angus beef should not be confused with prime. Though it is a high grade choice cut, it does not have the texture or taste of prime. When purchasing sirloin strip steaks, look for light consistent marbling and rich red color. Ribeyes should have the same marbling and color. The thick fat line should roll into the center of the steak and not meet at the top. The latter indicates an end cut and ultimately a tougher cut. The filet mignon, center cut from the beef tenderloin, should be one solid barrel of beef uninterrupted with marble or fat. This indicates that it is not a butterflied head or tail cut, but a true center cut filet. All of these steaks should be firm to the touch. Avoid steaks with a deep ruby red color that are soft to the touch. This meat was probably packed one to two weeks earlier than it should have been, not allowing for proper drying and aging.

Veal should be a soft pink color and firm. Milk fed baby veal is the ideal product for veal medallions or chops. Many restaurants boast of using veal shortloins. This is the most expensive cut of veal available, but I feel not necessarily the most tender or tasteful. I prefer to use a high quality sirloin butt or top round. Veal should be cooked in a very high temperature butter or olive oil, simply seasoned with salt and white pepper and dusted lightly with white flour.

A great roasted chicken is a tremendous culinary success. Fresh, whole chickens are oven roasted with herbs and garlic to obtain a crisp skin and tender juicy meat. Sounds simple, but when was the last time you had a memorable roasted chicken? Boneless domestic ducks are roasted and served with an assortment of sauces.

Remember that meat and poultry products contain a wonderful natural flavor within waiting to be released. The seasoning and cooking method of these items should be geared towards complementing the natural flavor, not overpowering them.

Grilled Prime N.Y. Strip

4	14 ounce	N.Y. strip steak
	to taste	salt
	to taste	black pepper
	to taste	cayenne pepper
	to taste	paprika
	to taste	granulated garlic

Procedure:

• *Preheat a grill surface. (preferably an overhead broiler)*

Bring the steaks to room temperature and season to taste. Grill to desired doneness and serve immediately.
Serves 4

Prime N.Y. Strip Siciliano

4	14 ounce	N.Y. strip steak
	to taste	salt
	to taste	black pepper
	to taste	thyme, chopped
	to taste	basil, chopped
	to taste	garlic, chopped
1/2	pound	mozzarella, sliced
1/2	cup	Madeira wine
2	cup	veal stock
1/4	cup	sundried tomato, chopped

Procedure:

• *Preheat an oven to 500°. Season the strip steaks to taste with the herbs, salt and black pepper.*

Place the steaks in a roasting pan. Cook to the desired doneness. Remove the steaks from the roasting pan and keep warm.

Cover the steaks with the sliced mozzarella and chopped sun-dried tomatoes. Keep warm.

Place the roasting pan on a high fire and deglaze the pan with the Madeira wine. Add the veal stock and reduce to half the original volume. Serve the reduced sauce over the steaks.
Serves 4

Tenderloin of Beef with Green Peppercorn Sauce

4	8 ounce	filet
1/2	stick	butter
1/2	cup	brandy
1/4	cup	green peppercorn
2	cup	veal stock
1	cup	heavy cream
	to taste	salt

Procedure:

☐ *In a large sauté pan, melt the butter. Add the filets and cook to the desired doneness.*

Remove the steaks from the sauté pan. Deglaze the pan with the brandy. (Be cautious of the brandy igniting instantly if using a gas range.)

Add the green peppercorns, veal stock and heavy cream. Reduce to half the original volume. Season to taste with salt.

Return the filets to the pan to reheat.

Serve the filets topped with the green peppercorn sauce.
Serves 4

Crushed Pepper Steak

4	14 ounce	N.Y. strip steak
1	cup	black peppercorn, whole
1/2	stick	butter
1/2	cup	brandy
2	cup	veal stock
1	cup	heavy cream
	to taste	salt

Procedure:

☐ *Place the black peppercorns on a cutting board. Using the bottom of a sauté pan crush the peppercorns by rolling the pan over them while applying pressure.*

Press the strip steaks into the peppercorns, coating both sides.

Melt the butter in a large sauté pan and cook the steaks to the desired doneness.

Remove the steaks from the sauté pan and keep warm.

Deglaze the pan with brandy. (Be cautious of the brandy igniting instantly if using a gas range.)

Add the veal stock and heavy cream. Reduce to half the original volume. Season the sauce to taste with salt.

Return the steaks to the pan to reheat. Serve the strip steaks topped with the reduced sauce.
Serves 4

Beef Tenderloin with Roquefort Sauce

4	8 ounce	filet
1/2	stick	butter
1/2	cup	brandy
1/2	cup	Roquefort cheese, crumbled
2	cup	veal stock
1	cup	heavy cream
	to taste	salt
	to taste	white pepper

Procedure:

• *Season the filets to taste with salt and white pepper. In a large sauté pan, melt the butter. Cook the filets to the desired doneness and remove from the sauté pan. Keep warm.*

Add the cheese to the sauté pan and deglaze the pan with brandy. (Be cautious of the brandy igniting instantly if using a gas range.)

Add the veal stock and heavy cream. Reduce to half the original volume. Adjust the seasonings if necessary.

Return the steaks to the pan to be reheated. Serve topped with the reduced sauce.
Serves 4

Grilled Ribeye Steak with Bordelaise Sauce

4	14 ounce	ribeye steak
3	cup	veal stock
1/2	cup	red wine
1/4	cup	brandy
2	tablespoon	garlic, chopped
1	tablespoon	thyme, chopped
1/2	cup	Italian plum tomato, crushed
	to taste	black pepper

Procedure:

• *Preheat a grill surface. Season the ribeye steaks to taste.*

Place all of the remaining ingredients in a sauce pot and reduce to half the original volume. Season to taste with black pepper.

Grill the ribeye steaks to the desired doneness and served topped with the reduced bordelaise sauce.

Serves 4

Beef Tenderloin Medallions with Jumbo Shrimp

8	4 ounce	filet medallion
1/2	stick	butter
	to taste	salt
	to taste	white pepper
8	jumbo	shrimp, peeled
1	portion	meuniere sauce (see page 39)
1	portion	hollandaise sauce (see page 39)
1	tablespoon	tarragon leaf
1	teaspoon	garlic, chopped
	to taste	black pepper

Procedure:

• *Prepare the meuniere sauce. Prepare the hollandaise sauce and blend in the tarragon leaves and garlic. Season to taste with black pepper. Keep warm.*

Season the filet medallions to taste with salt and white pepper. Melt the butter in a large sauté pan.

Sauté the medallions to the desired doneness and remove from the pan. Keep warm.

Add the shrimp to the pan and sauté until the shrimp are cooked thoroughly.

Place 2 filet medallions on each plate and top the pair with the meuniere sauce. Top each medallion with a sautéed shrimp. Top the shrimp with the prepared bearnaise sauce.
Serves 4

Beef Tenderloin Medallions with Crawfish Tails

8	4 ounce	filet medallion
1/2	stick	butter
	to taste	salt
	to taste	white pepper
2	cup	veal stock
2	cup	red wine
1	portion	hollandaise sauce (see page 39)
1	tablespoon	tarragon leaf
1	teaspoon	garlic, chopped
	to taste	black pepper
1/2	stick	butter, melted
1/2	pound	crawfish tail
1/2	cup	green onion, chopped
2	teaspoon	lemon juice

Procedure:

• *Prepare the hollandaise sauce and blend in the tarragon leaves and garlic. Season to taste with black pepper. Keep warm.*

Season the filet medallions to taste with salt and white pepper. Melt a 1/2 stick of butter in a large sauté pan.

Saute the filet medallions to the desired doneness. Remove from the sauté pan and keep warm.

Deglaze the pan with the red wine. Add the veal stock and reduce to half the original volume. Keep warm.

Sauté the crawfish tails in a 1/2 stick melted butter with the green onions and lemon juice. Season to taste with salt and white pepper.

Reheat the filet medallions in the reduced sauce. Transfer 2 medallions to each dinner plate. Top with the reduced red wine sauce.

Top each pair of filet medallions with 2 ounces of sautéed crawfish tails. Top the crawfish tails with the prepared bearnaise sauce.
Serves 4

Marinated, Grilled Fajita Steak with Corn Relish

1	2 pound	flank steak
1/2	cup	canola oil
1/4	cup	soy sauce
2	tablespoon	lime juice
1	tablespoon	garlic, chopped
1	tablespoon	black pepper
1	cup	sour cream

• Corn Relish

1	can	corn
1		red onion, diced
1		tomato, diced
1		jalapeno, diced
1/2	bunch	cilantro, chopped
2	tablespoon	honey
	to taste	salt

Procedures:

• Flank Steak
Marinate the flank steak in the canola oil, soy sauce, lime juice, garlic and black pepper for at least 1 hour, turning periodically.

Preheat a grill surface.

• Corn Relish
Prepare the relish by combining all of the ingredients in a mixing bowl and season to taste with salt. Let stand 30 minutes.

Grill the fajita steak to desired doneness and slice thinly across the grain. Serve garnished with the sour cream and prepared relish.
Serves 4

Veal Marina

8	3 ounce	veal medallion, pounded thin
1	stick	butter
		white flour
	to taste	salt
	to taste	white pepper
2	teaspoon	garlic, chopped
1	cup	mushroom, sliced
1	tablespoon	parsley, chopped
1/4	cup	white wine
1	portion	meuniere sauce (see page 39)
1	portion	hollandaise sauce (see page 39)
1	tablespoon	tarragon leaf
	to taste	black pepper
1/2	pound	crawfish tail
1/2	pound	crabmeat
1/4	cup	green onion, chopped

Procedure:

Prepare the meuniere sauce and the hollandaise sauce. Prepare the bearnaise sauce by adding 1 teaspoon of garlic, tarragon leaves and black pepper to taste to the hollandaise sauce. Keep warm.

Melt a 1/2 stick of butter in a large sauté pan. Season the veal medallions to taste with salt and white pepper. Dust the medallions with white flour shaking off all of the excess.

Sauté the veal in the melted butter, browning each side. Remove the medallions from the pan and keep warm.

Add the mushrooms, 1 teaspoon garlic and parsley to the sauté pan. Cook for 5 minutes. Add the white wine and reduce for 3 minutes. Remove from the heat and incorporate the meuniere sauce.

Melt a 1/2 stick of butter in a sauté pan. Add the crawfish tails, crabmeat and green onions. Sauté the crawfish tails and crabmeat until heated thoroughly. Season to taste with salt and white pepper.

Place 2 veal medallions on each plate and top with the mushroom sauce. Top each pair of veal medallions with crawfish and crabmeat and finish with the bearnaise sauce.

Serves 4

Veal Medallions with Garlic, Lemon and Capers

8	3 ounce	veal medallion, pounded thin
3/4	stick	butter
	to taste	salt
	to taste	white pepper
		white flour
1	tablespoon	garlic, chopped
1/4	cup	white wine
2	tablespoon	lemon juice
1/4	cup	chicken stock
3	tablespoon	caper
1	tablespoon	parsley, chopped
	to taste	black pepper

Procedure:

• Melt the butter in a large sauté pan. Season the veal medallions to taste with salt and white pepper. Dredge the veal medallions in the white flour. Do not shake off the excess flour.

Sauté the veal until brown on both sides. Remove from the pan and keep warm.

Add all of the remaining ingredients to the pan and reduce the sauce until it becomes thick. Season to taste with salt and black pepper.

Serve the veal medallions in pairs topped with the reduced sauce.

Serves 4

Veal Medallions with Rosemary Citrus Sauce

8	3 ounce	veal medallion, pounded thin
1/2	stick	butter
	to taste	salt
	to taste	white pepper
		white flour
1	tablespoon	rosemary, chopped
1	teaspoon	garlic, chopped
1/4	cup	chicken stock
1/4	cup	orange juice
1	tablespoon	lime juice
1	tablespoon	lemon juice

Procedure: • Melt the butter in a large sauté pan. Season the veal medallions to taste with salt and white pepper. Dust the medallions with white flour. Do not shake off the excess flour.

Sauté the veal until brown on both sides. Remove and keep warm.

Add all of the remaining ingredients and reduce the sauce until it is thick.

Serve the veal medallions in pairs topped with the reduced sauce.
Serves 4

Roasted Veal Loin Chop

4	12 ounce	veal loin chop
1/2	stick	butter
	to taste	salt
	to taste	white pepper
1		egg
1	cup	milk
		bread crumb
1	cup	red wine
3	cup	veal stock

Procedure: • Preheat an oven to 450°. Season the veal chops to taste with salt and white pepper.

Blend the egg and milk together thoroughly. Dip the veal chops in the milk wash and then into bread crumbs. Coat both sides and all of the edges.

Melt the butter in a roasting pan. Place the veal chops in the roasting pan and transfer to the oven.

Cook the veal chops for 7 minutes on each side. Remove the chops from the pan and keep warm.

Deglaze the pan with red wine and add the veal stock. Reduce to half the original volume.

Serve the veal chops topped with the reduced sauce.
Serves 4

Stuffed Veal Loin Chop with Sundried Tomato Sauce

4	12 ounce	veal loin chop
1/2	stick	butter
	to taste	salt
	to taste	white pepper
1		egg
1	cup	milk
		bread crumb
4	1 ounce	proscuitto, slice
4	1 ounce	fontina cheese, slice
2	tablespoon	sundried tomato, chopped
1	teaspoon	garlic, chopped
1	cup	Madeira wine
3	cup	veal stock

Procedure:

• *Preheat an oven to 450°. Cut a pocket in the veal loin chops extending from the outer edge of the meat to the bone.*

Roll the fontina cheese inside the sliced proscuitto. Stuff the fontina cheese and proscuitto in the pocket of the veal chops.

Season the veal chops to taste with salt and white pepper. (Consider the high salt content in the tomatoes and proscuitto when seasoning.)

Melt the butter in a roasting pan. Blend the egg and milk together thoroughly. Dip the stuffed veal chop in the milk wash and then into the bread crumbs. Coat both sides and all of the edges.

Place the veal chops in the roasting pan and cook for 8 minutes on each side. Remove the chops from the pan and keep warm.

Deglaze the pan with the Madeira wine. Add the sundried tomatoes, garlic and veal stock. Reduce to half the original volume.

Serve the veal chops topped with the reduced sauce.
Serves 4

Osso Bucca

6	3 inch thick	veal shank
	to taste	salt
	to taste	white pepper
1/4	cup	thyme, chopped
1/4	cup	garlic, clove
2	cup	Italian plum tomato, crushed
2		carrot, diced
1		yellow onion, diced
1		potato, diced
2		zucchini, diced
2		yellow squash, diced
2	cup	red wine
2	cup	veal stock

Procedure:

● *Preheat an oven to 450°. Season the veal shanks to taste with salt and white pepper. Place the shanks in a roasting pan.*

Add the thyme, garlic, tomato, onion and vegetables. Cook for 45 minutes or until the meat and vegetables are brown. Add 1 cup of the red wine and cover the roasting pan with aluminum foil.

Cook for an additional hour or until the meat pulls away from the bones easily.

Place the roasting pan on a high fire, remove the foil and add the remaining red wine and veal stock.

Reduce the sauce to the desired consistency. Season to taste with salt and white pepper.

Serve the veal shanks topped with the vegetables and reduced sauce.

Serves 6

Roasted Rack of Lamb with Vegetables

2	8 chop	domestic lamb rack
1/4	cup	olive oil
	to taste	salt
	to taste	black pepper
2	tablespoon	rosemary, chopped
1	tablespoon	garlic, chopped
8		baby carrot, split
8		new potato, split
8		brussel sprout, split
1		yellow onion, diced large
2		yellow squash, diced large
2		roma tomato, quartered
1	cup	red wine
2	cup	lamb stock

Procedure:

• *Preheat an oven to 450°. Brush the lamb racks with olive oil, rosemary and chopped garlic. Season to taste with salt and black pepper.*

Toss all of the vegetables in olive oil and season to taste with salt and black pepper.

Place the lamb and vegetables in a roasting pan. Cook the lamb to the desired doneness. Remove the racks from the roasting pan and keep warm.

Allow the vegetables to cook until brown and tender. Remove from the roasting pan and keep warm.

Place the pan on a high fire and deglaze the pan with red wine. Add the lamb stock and reduce until thick. Season to taste with salt and black pepper.

Slice the lamb racks into chops and serve with the roasted vegetables and reduced sauce.

Serves 4

Grilled Lamb Loin Chops with Dijon® Mustard Sauce

8	6 ounce	domestic lamb loin chop
	to taste	salt
	to taste	black pepper
2	cup	lamb stock
1/2	cup	Dijon® mustard
1	cup	heavy cream
1	teaspoon	lemon juice

Procedure: ▪ *Preheat a grill surface. Season the lamb chops to taste with salt and black pepper.*

In a sauce pot, combine the lamb stock, Dijon® mustard, heavy cream and lemon juice. Reduce the sauce until thick, stirring with a whip periodically.

Grill the lamb loin chops to the desired doneness and serve topped with the reduced sauce.
Serves 4

Grilled Lamb Loin Chops, Garlic and Mint Sauce

8	6 ounce	domestic lamb loin chop
	to taste	salt
	to taste	black pepper
3	cup	lamb stock
1	cup	red wine
1	tablespoon	garlic, chopped
1	tablespoon	mint, chopped

Procedure: ▪ *Preheat a grill surface. Season the lamb loin chops to taste with salt and black pepper.*

In a sauce pot, combine the lamb stock, red wine, garlic, mint and black pepper to taste. Reduce the sauce until thick.

Grill the lamb chops to the desired doneness and serve topped with the reduced sauce.
Serves 4

Grilled Pork Loin Steak with Proscuitto and Fontina Cheese

4	12 ounce	pork loin steak
		olive oil
	to taste	salt
	to taste	white pepper
4	1 ounce	proscuitto slice
4	2 ounce	fontina cheese slice
3	cup	veal stock
1	cup	Madeira wine
1	tablespoon	rosemary, chopped

Procedure:

• Preheat a grill surface. Brush the pork steaks with olive oil and season to taste with salt and white pepper.

Grill the pork steaks to the desired doneness. While the steaks are grilling, reduce the veal stock and Madeira wine to half the original volume.

Place a slice of proscuitto and fontina cheese on top of each pork steak. Let the steaks remain on the grill long enough to heat the proscuitto and melt the cheese.

Remove the steaks from the grill and serve topped with the reduced sauce and garnish with chopped rosemary.
Serves 4

Grilled Pork Loin Chop with Apple and Ginger Sauce

4	12 ounce	pork loin chop
	to taste	salt
	to taste	white pepper
		white flour
1/2	stick	butter
2		Granny Smith apple, diced
2	tablespoon	crystallized ginger, chopped fine
1	large	yellow onion, diced
1	teaspoon	garlic, chopped
	to taste	crushed red pepper
1/4	cup	white wine
1	cup	chicken stock

Procedure: • *Preheat an oven to 450˚. Season the pork chops to taste with salt and white pepper. Dredge the chops in white flour.*

Melt the butter in a large sauté pan. Place the pork chops in the sauté pan and brown lightly on both sides. Transfer the sauté pan to the oven.

Cook the pork chops to the desired doneness and remove from the pan and keep warm.

Add 1 tablespoon of white flour to the pan drippings and blend in thoroughly. Add the apples, ginger, yellow onions and garlic. Sauté for 3 minutes.

Add the white wine and chicken stock and reduce until thick. Season to taste with salt and crushed red pepper.

Serve the pork chops topped with the reduced sauce.
Serves 4

Roasted Chicken with Garlic and Vegetables

2	whole	chicken, split
	to taste	salt
	to taste	granulated garlic
	to taste	cayenne pepper
1/2	cup	parsley, chopped
2	tablespoon	rosemary, chopped
10	clove	garlic
2		carrot, cut into 1 inch segments
2		baking potato, diced large
1/2	cup	olive oil
1/2	cup	white wine
1	tablespoon	lemon juice
2	cup	water

Procedure: • *Preheat an oven to 425˚. Season the chickens to taste with salt, garlic and cayenne pepper.*

Place the chickens in a roasting pan with all of the remaining ingredients except the parsley.

Roast the chickens for 30 minutes or until brown and crisp and clear juice runs from a pricked thigh.

Remove the chickens from the roasting pan and keep warm. Reduce the sauce with the vegetables until thick.

Serve the chickens with the roasted vegetables, reduced sauce and garnish with chopped parsley.
Serves 4

Roasted Chicken with Mushrooms and Marsala Wine

2	whole	chicken, split
	to taste	salt
	to taste	black pepper
1	pound	mushroom, sliced
1	tablespoon	garlic, chopped
1	cup	Marsala wine
1/2	cup	parsley, chopped
2	cup	chicken stock

Procedure:

▣ *Preheat an oven to 425°. Season the chickens to taste with salt and black pepper.*

Place the chickens in a roasting pan and cook for 30 minutes or until brown and crisp and clear juice runs from a pricked thigh.

Remove the chickens from the pan and keep warm. Add the garlic, mushrooms and parsley to the pan drippings and sauté for 3 minutes.

Add the Marsala wine and chicken stock. Reduce the sauce until thick. Serve over the roasted chickens.
Serves 4

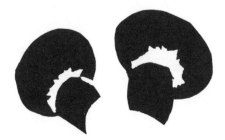

Stuffed Cornish Hens with Crystallized Ginger Glaze

4		cornish hen
2		carrot, diced
1		yellow onion, diced
1		potato, diced
to taste		salt
to taste		white pepper

Recipe by
Chef Sonny Creel

• Stuffing

1/2	head	bok choy cabbage
1		green onion, chopped
	pinch	garlic, chopped
2	ounce	peanut oil
2	teaspoon	rice vinegar
1/2		yellow onion, diced
8	strip	bacon, chopped

• Glaze

1/2	cup	soy sauce
1/4	cup	sugar
1	teaspoon	black pepper
1/2	teaspoon	salt
1/4	cup	orange juice
1/4	teaspoon	granulated garlic
3	tablespoon	crystallized ginger, chopped

Procedures:

• Stuffing
Sauté the bok choy, onions and bacon in oil on high heat. Finish with garlic and vinegar. Cool and stuff into the hens.

• Glaze
Blend all of the ingredients in a bowl and mix well.

• Cornish Hen
Preheat an oven to 350°. Place the carrots, onions and potatoes in a roasting pan with a little water. Season the hens to taste with salt and white pepper. Place the hens on top of the vegetables.

Cook the hens until the legs turn freely. Brush the hens with the glaze and roast an additional 5 minutes.

Serve the hens over the roasted vegetables with additional glaze.
Serves 4

Crispy Boneless Duck

2	5 pound	duck
		soy sauce
	to taste	salt
	to taste	granulated garlic
	to taste	black pepper
1	large	yellow onion
2		carrot
2	rib	celery
1	head	garlic, split

Procedure:

• Preheat an oven to 400°. Trim the ducks of all excess fat and remove the organs from the chest cavity.

Coarsely chop all of the vegetables and stuff into the chest cavities.

Brush the ducks with soy sauce and season heavily with salt, granulated garlic and black pepper.

Place the ducks on a wire rack in a roasting pan and cook for 1 1/2 hours. The ducks should be brown and crisp.

Check the duck by turning the legs. If they move freely, the ducks are finished. Remove the ducks and allow to cool.

Split the ducks and remove the bones from the inside. Cut the skin that surrounds the leg and wing bones and pull these bones out from the inside.

Trim all of the excess skin and fat.

Prepare a duck sauce. See recipe selections on page 141.

Place the deboned ducks meat side down in a roasting pan. Reheat the ducks in a 500° oven and serve with prepared duck sauce.
Serves 4

Natural Duck Sauce

3	cup	duck stock
1	cup	Madeira wine

Procedure: • *In the roasting pan used to finish the boneless ducks, add the Madeira wine and duck stock. Reduce to half the original volume.*

Serve over the roasted ducks.
Serves 4

Green Peppercorn Duck Sauce

3	cup	duck stock
1	cup	Madeira wine
1/2	cup	green peppercorn

Procedure: • *In the roasting pan used to finish the boneless ducks, add the Madeira wine, peppercorns and duck stock. Reduce to half the original volume.*

Serve over the roasted ducks.
Serves 4

Raspberry Duck Sauce

3	cup	duck stock
1/2	cup	Madeira wine
1/4	cup	sugar
3/4	cup	raspberry

Procedure: • *In the roasting pan used to finish the boneless ducks, add the Madeira wine, raspberries, sugar and duck stock. Reduce to half the original volume.*

Strain through a fine sieve or chinois. Serve over the roasted ducks.
Serves 4

Oriental Mango Duck with Tempura Onions

2	5 pound	duck
1/2	cup	soy sauce
	to taste	salt
	to taste	granulated garlic
	to taste	black pepper
2	tablespoon	five spice
2	large	yellow onion
1		carrot
2	rib	celery
2	head	garlic, split
1	tablespoon	red miso sauce
1		mango, peeled, seeded and pureed
1	tablespoon	sugar
2	cup	duck stock
4		green onion, tempura battered and fried

Procedure:

- *Follow the procedures for the roasted duck on page 140 with the addition of the Chinese five spice for seasoning the skin.*

  In the roasting pan used to finish the boneless ducks, add the remaining soy sauce, mango puree, red miso, sugar and duck stock.

  Reduce the sauce until thick and serve over the duck. Garnish with the tempura, fried whole green onions.
  Serves 4

Sautéed Duck Breast with Banana Sauce

4	8 ounce	duck breast
1/4	stick	butter
	to taste	salt
	to taste	white pepper
1/2	cup	banana liqueur
1	tablespoon	sugar
1		egg yolk
1	cup	heavy cream
1		banana, pureed
2	cup	duck stock

Procedure: • *Pound the duck breast thin with a meat hammer. Season to taste with salt and white pepper.*

Melt the butter in a sauté pan and cook the duck breast to the desired doneness. Remove from the pan and keep warm.

Blend the egg yolk, cream and pureed banana together with a wire whip.

Deglaze the pan with the banana liqueur. (Be cautious of the liqueur igniting instantly if using a gas range.)

Add the sugar, duck stock and cream mixture, stirring continuously while incorporating the cream mixture.

Reduce the sauce to half the original volume and serve over the sautéed duck breast.
Serves 4

Fried Turkey

1		turkey
	to taste	salt
	to taste	granulated garlic
	to taste	black pepper
	to taste	paprika
4	gallon	peanut oil

Procedure: • *In a 10 gallon pot or large deep fryer, heat the peanut oil to 350°.*

Season the turkey heavily inside and out.

Fry the turkey for 5 minutes per each pound. Turn the turkey once during the total cooking time.

Remove the turkey from the fryer and let drain for 15 minutes on paper towels or a cooling rack. Slice and serve immediately.
Serve 1 pound (raw weight) per person

Game

Avid hunters often have full freezers after a successful hunting season. The recipes in this section offer simple suggestions for preparing the prized game. The spoils of the hunt will no longer linger with ice cube trays, vanilla ice cream and the two hot dogs left over from the ten-pack that did not fit the eight-pack buns.

It is not necessary to be a hunter in order to enjoy wild game. Quail, rabbit, venison, duck and pheasant are frequently available commercially.

Farm raised products lack many of the negative characteristics that diners often find distasteful. Some of the items in this section may be difficult to locate. However, when the opportunity presents itself, take full advantage of wild game choices. I think you will be pleasantly surprised.

Game adapts well to all cuisine and cooking methods. Create a hearty court-bouillon or jambalaya with almost any game. Roasted with vegetables and served with natural juices or sautéed and served with delicate sauces, wild game will rival the best of beef and veal dishes.

The preparation of wild game need not be intimidating. Proper cooking times and technique will keep the hunter in the woods, the cook in the kitchen and the guest delighted.

Boneless Quails Stuffed with Andouille Rice

8		boneless quail
1/4	cup	butter, melted
	to taste	salt
	to taste	white pepper
1	portion	andouille rice (see page 115)
1/4	cup	Worcestershire sauce
1/4	cup	honey
3	cup	duck stock

Procedure:

• *Preheat an oven to 400°. Prepare the andouille rice and cool.*

Stuff each quail with andouille rice and bring the legs together. Secure with a toothpick.

Place the quails in a roasting pan. Top each quail with melted butter and season to taste with salt and white pepper.

Roast the quails in the oven for 20 minutes. Remove from the oven and take the quails out of the roasting pan. Keep warm.

Place the roasting pan on a medium fire. Add the Worcestershire sauce, honey and duck stock to the pan drippings.

Reduce the sauce until thick. Remove the toothpicks from the quails and serve them in pairs with the reduced honey Worcestershire sauce.
Serves 4

Boneless Quails Stuffed with Oysters

8		boneless quail
1/4	cup	butter, melted
	to taste	salt
	to taste	white pepper
1/2	cup	onion, diced
1/4	cup	celery, diced
1/4	cup	bell pepper, diced
1	tablespoon	garlic, chopped
1	cup	oyster
1	tablespoon	sherry
1	teaspoon	lemon juice

		bread crumb
1	cup	morel mushroom, sliced
1/4	cup	brandy
2	cup	duck stock
1	cup	cream

Procedure:

- In a food processor combine the onions, celery, bell pepper, garlic, oysters, sherry and lemon juice. Puree.

  Add the bread crumbs to the pureed mixture until firm but not dry. Season to taste with salt and white pepper.

  Preheat an oven to 400°. Stuff each quail with oyster stuffing and bring the legs together, securing with toothpicks.

  Place the quails in a roasting pan. Top each quail with melted butter and season to taste with salt and white pepper.

  Roast the quails in the oven for 20 minutes. Remove from the oven and take the quails out of the roasting pan. Keep warm.

  Place the roasting pan on a medium fire and add the brandy, morel mushrooms, duck stock and cream to the pan drippings.

  Reduce the sauce until thick. Season to taste with salt and white pepper. Remove the toothpicks from the quails and serve them in pairs with the reduced morel mushroom sauce.

  Serves 4

Broiled Quails with Spinach and Raspberry Sauce

4		boneless quail, split lengthwise
1/2	cup	butter, melted
2	tablespoon	sugar
	to taste	salt
	to taste	white pepper
1	pound	spinach
2	tablespoon	salad oil
1	tablespoon	soy sauce
1	pint	raspberry
3	tablespoon	butter
1	tablespoon	brown sugar
2	tablespoon	honey
1	cup	water

Recipe by Chef John Adams

Procedure: • Cook the raspberries for 5 minutes in the water. Drain.

In a sauté pan melt 2 tablespoons of butter. Add the sugar, raspberries and honey. Simmer this mixture for 2 minutes or until thick. Keep warm.

Preheat a broiler. Brush the quails with melted butter and season to taste with salt and white pepper.

Place the quails in the broiler breast side down. Cook the quails for 5 minutes. Turn and cook an additional 8 minutes brushing the quails with butter periodically.

Remove the quails and keep warm.

Wash and dry the spinach. Remove the stems and cut into 1 inch segments. Heat the oil and soy sauce in a sauté pan.

Add the spinach and cook for 1 minute or until completely wilted.

Place the spinach on the base of 4 dinner plates. Place the quails on top of the spinach and finish with the raspberry glaze.
Serves 4

Sautéed Rabbit with Sweet Tomato Sauce

1		rabbit, quartered
1	rib	celery, diced
1		onion, diced
1	clove	garlic, minced
1	tablespoon	parsley, chopped
1/2	cup	salad oil
3	cup	tomato, crushed
2	teaspoon	salt
1/4	cup	milk
1/4	cup	honey
1	cup	white flour
1/4	teaspoon	black pepper

Recipe by
Chef Troy "Slim" Klamerus

Procedure: ▪ *Sauté the onions, garlic, celery tomato, parsley and a 1/2 teaspoon of salt in a sauté pan for 10 minutes.*

Combine the milk and honey. Dip the rabbit into the milk mixture.

Roll the rabbit in the white flour, salt and black pepper. Heat the oil in a sauté pan and brown the rabbit on both sides.

Add the sauce and tomato juice. Cover and simmer for 1 hour. Serve the rabbit topped with the sauce.
Serves 4

Hot and Sour Rabbit with Napa Cabbage and Sweet Peppers

2		rabbit, deboned
	to taste	salt
	to taste	white pepper
1	head	Napa cabbage, shredded
1		red sweet pepper, diced coarse
1		gold sweet pepper, diced coarse
1/4	cup	canola oil
2	portion	hot and sour dressing (see page 67)

Procedure: ▪ *Prepare the dressing. Cut the deboned rabbit into bite size pieces.*

Heat the canola oil in a sauté pan and season the rabbit to taste with salt and white pepper.

Sauté the rabbit until cooked thoroughly. Remove the rabbit meat from the pan and keep warm. Add the Napa cabbage and sauté for 3 minutes.

Remove the Napa cabbage from the sauté pan and place the cabbage on the base of 4 dinner plates.

Return the rabbit to the sauté pan with the sweet peppers and sauté for 1 minute. Add the dressing and sauté until thoroughly heated.

Serve the rabbit mixture over the sautéed Napa cabbage.
Serves 4

Grilled Rabbit with Southwestern Style Barbecue Sauce

2		rabbit, quartered
1/2	cup	butter, melted
	to taste	salt
	to taste	black pepper
1	cup	onion, chopped
1/3	cup	bell pepper, chopped
1/3	cup	celery, chopped
1/3	cup	parsley, chopped
1/3	cup	canola oil
1	tablespoon	garlic, chopped
1/4	cup	Worcestershire sauce
1		jalapeno, diced
2	cup	ketchup
1/2	cup	cilantro, chopped
1	tablespoon	cumin

Procedure:

• Heat the canola oil in a sauce pot and sauté the onions, bell pepper, celery and garlic for 10 minutes.

Add the ketchup, Worcestershire sauce, parsley, cilantro, jalapeno, cumin and season to taste with salt and black pepper.

Remove the barbecue sauce from the heat and set aside.

Preheat a grill surface. Brush the rabbit pieces with the melted butter and season to taste with salt and black pepper.

Grill the rabbit pieces, brushing with barbecue sauce during the cooking process.

Remove the cooked rabbit from the grill and serve with additional barbecue sauce.

Serves 4

Grilled Venison Sausage with Caramelized Onions

4	pound	boneless pork meat
5	pound	boneless venison meat
10	large	yellow onion
3	bunch	green onion
1	cup	garlic clove
1/2	cup	thyme
	to taste	salt
	to taste	black pepper
	to taste	cayenne pepper
1/2	stick	butter

Procedure:

- *Cube the pork and venison into 1 inch pieces. Peel 5 of the onions and coarsely chop. Remove the green onion bottoms and coarsely chop.*

  Run all of the ingredients through a meat grinder with a medium to large grinding plate. Begin with the meat products and finish with the vegetables and herbs, followed by a small piece of bread to clear the remaining ingredients from the grinder.

  In a mixing bowl, blend all of the ingredients thoroughly and season to taste with salt, black pepper and cayenne pepper by cooking small patties to adjust seasonings.

  Form into 4 ounce patties or stuff into sausage casings.

  Julienne the 5 remaining onions. Melt the butter in a sauté pan and cook the onions until brown. Season to taste with salt and black pepper.

  Preheat a grill surface. Grill the sausage links or patties and serve with the caramelized onions and your favorite sweet mustard.

  This recipe makes approximately 10 pounds of sausage which freezes well.

  Serves 10

Grilled Venison Chops with Shiitake Mushrooms

4		venison loin chop
	to taste	salt
	to taste	granulated garlic
	to taste	black pepper
1/4	stick	butter
1/2	pound	shiitake mushroom
2	cup	red wine
3	cup	veal stock

Procedure: • *Preheat a grill surface. Season the venison chops with salt, granulated garlic and black pepper to taste.*

Clean and slice the shiitake mushrooms. Melt the butter in a sauté pan and cook the shiitake mushrooms for 5 minutes.

Add the red wine and veal stock and reduce to half the original volume.

Grill the venison chops to the desired doneness and serve topped with the reduced sauce.
Serves 4

Mustard Crusted Venison Medallions, Tuscan White Bean Sauce

8	3 ounce	venison tenderloin medallion, pounded thin
1/2	stick	butter
1/2	cup	white flour
1/2	cup	mustard, coarse ground
		bread crumb
1	portion	Tuscan white bean (see page 77)

Procedure: • *Prepare the beans. Finish the beans with a 1/2 cup of water and puree 1/2 of the mixture to give the beans a sauce-like texture.*

Dredge the venison medallions in the white flour and coat them with the mustard. Press the medallions into the bread crumbs.

Melt the butter in a sauté pan and cook the medallions to the desired doneness. Heat the white bean sauce and serve with the sautéed venison medallions.
Serves 4

Medallions of Venison with Dijon® Mustard Sauce

8	3 ounce	venison tenderloin medallion, pounded thin
1/2	stick	butter
	to taste	salt
	to taste	white pepper
		white flour
1/4	cup	white wine
1/4	cup	Dijon® mustard
2	cup	veal stock
1	cup	heavy cream

Procedure:

• Season the venison medallions with salt and white pepper. Dredge the venison in the white flour and shake off all of the excess flour.

Melt the butter in a sauté pan. Sauté the venison medallions to the desired doneness. Remove from the pan and keep warm.

Deglaze the pan with the white wine. Add the veal stock, Dijon® mustard and heavy cream. Reduce to half the original volume.

Serve the venison medallions in pairs topped with the reduced sauce.
Serves 4

Buffalo Tenderloin with Peppercorn Sauce and Carrot Chips

8	4 ounce	buffalo tenderloin medallion
1/2	stick	butter
	to taste	salt
	to taste	white pepper
1/4	cup	brandy
1/4	cup	green peppercorn
3	cup	veal stock
1	cup	heavy cream
1		carrot
1/4	cup	green onion, chopped

Procedure: • *Preheat a deep fryer to 375°.*

Peel the carrot and slice paper thin. Deep fry the carrot slices until brown. Transfer to a paper towel and let drain. Season to taste with salt and white pepper. Keep warm.

Melt the butter in a sauté pan. Season the buffalo to taste with salt and white pepper. Sauté the medallions to the desired doneness. Remove from the sauté pan and keep warm.

Deglaze the pan with the brandy. (Be cautious of the brandy igniting instantly if using a gas range.)

Add the peppercorns, veal stock and heavy cream. Reduce to half the original volume.

Serve the medallions in pairs topped with the reduced sauce, fried carrot chips and chopped green onions.
Serves 4

Buffalo Tenderloin, Caramelized Leeks and Portobello Mushrooms

8	4 ounce	buffalo tenderloin medallion
1	stick	butter
	to taste	salt
	to taste	white pepper
1	tablespoon	garlic, chopped
4		leek, chopped
4	large	portobello mushroom, quartered
1	cup	red wine
3	cup	veal stock

Procedure: • *Melt a 1/2 stick of butter in a sauté pan. Sauté the leeks with the garlic until brown. Season to taste with salt and white pepper.*

Season the medallions to taste with salt and white pepper. Melt the remaining butter in a sauté pan. Cook the buffalo to the desired doneness. Remove the medallions and keep warm.

Add the portobello mushrooms and sauté for 2 minutes. Deglaze the pan with red wine and add the veal stock. Reduce to half the original volume.

Serve the buffalo in pairs on top of leeks with the reduced sauce.
Serves 4

Grilled Buffalo Fajitas with Caramelized Onions and Pico de Gallo

4	14 ounce	buffalo strip steak
1/2	cup	canola oil
1/4	cup	soy sauce
2	tablespoon	lime juice
1	tablespoon	garlic, chopped
1	tablespoon	black pepper
1/2	stick	butter
3	large	yellow onion, julienned
	to taste	salt
	to taste	white pepper
1	cup	sour cream
1	portion	pico de gallo (see page 30)

Procedure: ● *Prepare the pico de gallo and chill.*

Marinate the strip steak in the canola oil, soy sauce, lime juice, garlic and black pepper for at least 1 hour. Turn periodically.

Melt the butter in a sauté pan and cook the onions until brown. Season to taste with salt and white pepper.

Preheat a grill surface. Grill the buffalo steaks to the desired doneness.

Place the caramelized onions on the base of 4 dinner plates. Slice the fajita steaks thinly across the grain.

Arrange the sliced buffalo on top of the caramelized onions. Top the fajitas with prepared pico de gallo and sour cream.
Serves 4

Buffalo Tenderloin Medallions with Mushroom Sauce

8	4 ounce	buffalo tenderloin medallion
1⁄2	stick	butter
	to taste	salt
	to taste	white pepper
1⁄2	pound	mushroom, sliced
2	tablespoon	garlic, chopped
2	tablespoon	brandy
1	cup	red wine
1⁄2	cup	green onion, chopped
1	cup	Italian plum tomato, crushed
2	cup	veal stock
	to taste	black pepper, coarse ground

Procedure:

■ Melt the butter in a sauté pan. Season the buffalo medallions to taste with salt and white pepper.

Sauté the buffalo to the desired doneness and remove from the pan. Keep warm.

Add the mushrooms and garlic. Sauté for 2 minutes.

Deglaze the pan with the brandy and red wine. (Be cautious of the brandy igniting instantly if using a gas range.)

Add the tomatoes, green onions and veal stock. Reduce the sauce to half the original volume.

Season the reduced sauce to taste with coarse ground black pepper.

Serve the buffalo medallions in pairs topped with the reduced mushroom sauce.

Serves 4

Sautéed Pheasant Breast with Tomato and Tarragon

4	6 ounce	pheasant breast, skinned and pounded
3	ounce	olive oil
	to taste	salt
	to taste	white pepper
1/2	cup	white flour
2	cup	Italian plum tomato, crushed
2	tablespoon	tarragon, chopped
1	tablespoon	garlic, chopped
2	ounce	white wine

Procedure: ▪ *Season the pheasant breast to taste with salt and white pepper. Dust the pheasant breast with white flour. Heat the olive oil in a sauté pan.*

Sauté the pheasant breast until brown on both sides. Add the crushed Italian tomatoes, garlic, tarragon and white wine.

Cook the pheasant with the sauce for 5 minutes. Season the sauce to taste with salt and white pepper.

Serve the pheasant with the reduced sauce.
Serves 4

Grilled Pheasant Breast with Braised Red Cabbage

4	6 ounce	pheasant breast, skinned and pounded
1/2	stick	butter, melted
	to taste	salt
	to taste	white pepper
1/2	head	red cabbage, shredded
1/2		apple, diced fine
1	tablespoon	garlic, chopped
2	tablespoon	sugar
1/4	cup	Worcestershire sauce
	to taste	black pepper

Procedure: ▪ *Preheat a grill surface. Season the pheasant breast to taste with salt and white pepper. Brush the pheasant breast with the butter.*

Grill the pheasant breast until thoroughly cooked. Remove from the grill and keep warm.

Sauté the red cabbage in the remaining butter with the diced apples, garlic and sugar. Season to taste with salt and black pepper. Sauté for 5 minutes.

Add the Worcestershire sauce to the cabbage mixture and sauté for 2 minutes. Serve with the grilled pheasant breast.
Serves 4

Sautéed Pheasant Breast with Morel Mushroom Sauce

4	6 ounce	pheasant breast, skinned and pounded
1/2	stick	butter
	to taste	salt
	to taste	white pepper
		white flour
1/4	cup	brandy
1/2	pound	morel mushroom
3	cup	chicken stock
1	cup	heavy cream

Procedure: ▪ *Season the pheasant breast to taste with salt and white pepper. Dust the pheasant breast with white flour.*

Melt the butter in a sauté pan. Sauté the pheasant breast until thoroughly cooked. Remove and keep warm.

Add the brandy. (Be cautious of the brandy igniting instantly if using a gas range.)

Add the morel mushrooms, chicken stock and heavy cream. Reduce the sauce to half the original volume. Season to taste with salt and white pepper.

Serve the reduced mushroom sauce with the pheasant breast.
Serves 4

Fish & Shellfish

Destin, Florida, situated in the heart of Florida's Gulf Coast, is known as "the luckiest fishing village in the world." For those of us who live along the Emerald Coast, a bounty of fresh gulf seafood is available throughout the year. For inland dwellers, fresh seafood might be somewhat more difficult to obtain. Fish and shellfish are healthy choices and are worth the search.

Grilling is a popular method of cooking seafood. I developed Chef's Grill Plus® with several culinary goals in mind. This unique product emphasizes the natural flavors and minimizes the frustration of grilling seafood. Fish will not stick to a grilling surface when lightly brushed with Chef's Grill Plus®.

Proper cooking time for boiled, sautéed, steamed and grilled seafood is a crucial element for successful preparation. Overcooked seafood tends to be dry, tough, and much of the natural flavor is lost.

In the preparation of seafood, freshness and the ability to determine freshness is vital. Smell is the determining factor in measuring the age of seafood. Normally, odor will be a sufficient indication of a seafood product's age.

However, frozen seafood products may be misleading. Frozen seafood tends to have a bland color and a broken, sponge-like texture. Determining the exact age of frozen seafood is virtually impossible. Unlike fish and crabmeat, shrimp and scallops freeze exceptionally well. When selecting seafood other than shrimp or scallops, I recommend purchasing fresh products.

Whole fish has built-in indicators for freshness or for the lack of freshness. The eyes will sink gradually into the head and turn a cloudy, white color as the fish ages. The gills will lose their rich, red color and their shape will deteriorate.

Although these general guidelines for selecting seafood are helpful, buying from a familiar source will insure quality, freshness and safety.

Fish and shellfish are abundant, healthy, and available in a wide price range. This section offers an eclectic assortment of my favorite signature fish and shellfish dishes.

Sautéed Red Snapper with Crabmeat

4	7 ounce	red snapper filet
1		egg
1/2	cup	milk
		white flour
	to taste	salt
	to taste	white pepper
1/2	cup	butter, melted
1	portion	meuniere sauce (see page 39)
1	portion	hollandaise sauce (see page 39)
1	pound	crabmeat
1/2	cup	green onion, chopped
1	tablespoon	lemon juice

Procedure: • *Prepare the meuniere and hollandaise sauces. Keep warm.*

Mix the egg and milk together thoroughly. Season the white flour to taste with salt and white pepper.

Preheat an oven to 450°. Heat a 1/4 cup of the melted butter in a sauté pan.

Dip the snapper filets in the egg and milk mixture. Dredge the filets through the white flour and shake off all of the excess flour.

Place the snapper filets in the sauté pan. Brown the filets on both sides and transfer the pan to the oven.

Bake the red snapper for 10 minutes and remove from the oven. Keep warm.

Heat the remaining melted butter in a sauté pan and add the crabmeat, lemon juice and green onions. Sauté the crabmeat until heated thoroughly. Season to taste with salt and white pepper.

Place the snapper filets on 4 dinner plates and top with the meuniere sauce. Place the sautéed crabmeat on top of the snapper. Top the crabmeat with the hollandaise sauce.

Serves 4

Grilled Red Snapper with Chive, Garlic Brown Butter Sauce

4	7 ounce	red snapper filet
		olive oil
	to taste	salt
	to taste	black pepper
2	stick	butter
1	tablespoon	garlic, chopped
2	tablespoon	lemon juice
1/4	cup	chive, chopped
	to taste	white pepper

Procedure:

- Preheat a grill surface. Brush the snapper filets with olive oil. Season the filets to taste with salt and black pepper.

Melt the butter in a sauté pan and cook until the butter turns a light brown color.

Add the lemon juice, garlic and chives. Remove from the fire and season to taste with salt and white pepper.

Grill the snapper filets until cooked thoroughly.

Place the snapper filets on 4 dinner plates and top with the brown butter sauce.
Serves 4

Grilled Grouper with Crabmeat and Crawfish Tails

4	7 ounce	grouper filet
		olive oil
	to taste	salt
	to taste	black pepper
1/2	portion	basil vinaigrette (see page 69)
1	portion	meuniere sauce (see page 39)
1/2	stick	butter
1/2	pound	crawfish tail
1/2	pound	crabmeat
1/2	cup	green onion, chopped
1	tablespoon	lemon juice
	to taste	white pepper

Procedure: • *Prepare the basil vinaigrette. Prepare the meuniere sauce.*

Preheat a grill surface. Preheat an oven to 450°.

Brush the grouper filets with olive oil and season to taste with salt and black pepper.

Place the grouper filets on the grill and mark both sides of the fish. Transfer the filets to a roasting pan.

Cover the filets with the basil vinaigrette. Place the roasting pan in the oven and bake the fish for 10 minutes. Remove and keep warm.

Melt the butter in a sauté pan. Add the crawfish, crabmeat, green onions and lemon juice. Sauté the crawfish and crabmeat until heated thoroughly. Season to taste with salt and white pepper.

Place the grouper filets on 4 dinner plates and top with the meuniere sauce. Top the filets with the sautéed crawfish and crabmeat mixture.
Serves 4

Grouper Baked in a Paper Bag

4	7 ounce	grouper filet
1	cup	baby shrimp
1/2	pound	asparagus
2	cup	heavy cream
1/2	cup	dry vermouth
1	tablespoon	lemon juice
1	teaspoon	garlic, chopped
	to taste	salt
	to taste	white pepper
4	sheet	parchment paper
1/2		red sweet pepper, diced

Procedure: • *Cut the bottoms off the asparagus and steam al denté. Cut the tips off the asparagus and reserve. Puree the bottoms in a food processor.*

In a sauté pan, reduce the cream with the dry vermouth, lemon juice, garlic and pureed asparagus to half the original volume. Season to taste with salt and white pepper.

Preheat an oven to 450°. Butter both sides of the parchment paper. Fold the paper in half and cut a half heart shaped figure in the paper. (The center of the heart should be at the fold in the paper.)

Unfold the paper to expose a full heart shaped figure. Place the grouper filet in the middle of one side of the paper heart.

Place a 1/4 cup of shrimp and the asparagus tips on the top of each filet. Pour a 1/4 cup of sauce over each filet and garnish with the diced red pepper.

Fold the opposite side of the paper heart over the top of the grouper to match the opposite edge. Begin at the top left corner making a series of small folds forming a sealed seam running the entire edge of the heart.

The seam will encase the grouper in a paper bag with a tail at the bottom which should be tucked under the bag.

Place the bags on a roasting pan and place in the preheated oven. Bake for 20 minutes or until the bag becomes filled with air and turns brown in color.

Remove the roasting pan from the oven and place the bags on 4 dinner plates. Serve immediately. (The bag should be cut open in front of the guest.)

Serves 4

Grouper Baked with Buster Crabs

4	7 ounce	grouper filet
4	baby	soft shell crab
	to taste	salt
	to taste	white pepper
1/4	cup	butter, melted
1	portion	basil vinaigrette (see page 69)
1/4	cup	dry sherry
2	tablespoon	lemon juice
2	tablespoon	paprika
1/2	cup	green onion, chopped

Procedure:

• *Prepare the basil vinaigrette.*

Clean the soft shell crabs by removing the lungs beneath the skin and trimming off the eyes and mouth.

Season the grouper and crabs with salt and white pepper. Place the cleaned crabs on top of the filets, the top sides of the crabs facing down.

Preheat an oven to 450°. Place the grouper filets topped with the crabs in a roasting pan.

Cover the filets and crabs with all of the remaining ingredients.

Transfer to the oven. Bake for 20 minutes and remove from the oven.

Place the baked grouper and crabs on 4 dinner plates and reduce the sauce formed in the pan until thick.

Serve the filets topped with the reduced sauce.

Serves 4

Grilled Grouper and Shrimp with Black Bean Sauce

4	7 ounce	grouper filet
8	jumbo	shrimp
		olive oil
	to taste	salt
	to taste	black pepper
1	portion	basil vinaigrette (see page 69)
1/4	portion	black bean soup (see page 29)
		water
1/2		red sweet pepper, diced
1/2		jalapeno, diced

Procedure:

• *Prepare the basil vinaigrette.*

Prepare the black bean soup and puree. Add enough water to the pureed soup to give it a sauce-like texture. Adjust the seasonings if necessary.

Preheat a grill surface. Brush the grouper filets and shrimp with olive oil. Season the filets and shrimp to taste with salt and black pepper.

Preheat an oven to 450°. Place the shrimp and grouper on the grill. Mark both sides of the shrimp and grouper.

Transfer the grouper to a roasting pan and place 2 shrimp on top of each filet. Cover the grouper and shrimp with the prepared basil vinaigrette.

Place the roasting pan in the oven and bake for 20 minutes. Remove from the oven.

Heat the black bean sauce and cover the base of 4 dinner plates. Place the grouper filets and shrimp on top of the black bean sauce.

Garnish the plates with the diced red sweet pepper and diced jalapeno.
Serves 4

Grilled Tuna with Braised Sea Scallops and Key Lime Butter

4	7 ounce	tuna steak
		olive oil
	to taste	salt
	to taste	black pepper
1/2	stick	butter
20	jumbo	sea scallop
1/4	cup	lime juice
1/2	cup	heavy cream
1/4	cup	white wine
1	teaspoon	lime peel, grated
2	stick	butter, chipped
	to taste	white pepper

Procedure:

• In a sauce pot, reduce the heavy cream, white wine, lime juice and lime peel to half the original volume.

Slowly whip in the chipped butter until all of the butter is incorporated. Season to taste with salt and white pepper. Keep warm.

Preheat a grill surface. Brush the scallops and tuna with the olive oil and season to taste with salt and black pepper.

Grill the scallops and tuna to the desired doneness. Remove from the grill.

Place the tuna steaks on the base of 4 dinner plates. Top the tuna with 5 sautéed scallops and finish with the key lime butter sauce.
Serves 4

Grilled Tuna with a Caramelized Tomato and Onion Vinaigrette

4	7 ounce	tuna steak
5	ounce	olive oil
	to taste	salt
	to taste	black pepper
2	large	yellow onion, julienned
1	cup	Italian plum tomato, crushed
1	tablespoon	garlic, chopped
2	tablespoon	butter, melted
2	tablespoon	balsamic vinegar

Procedure: • Heat the melted butter in a sauté pan. Add the julienned onions and sauté until the onions are brown.

Add the garlic and tomatoes and cook for 5 minutes.

Add the balsamic vinegar and 4 ounces of the olive oil. Season to taste with salt and black pepper. Keep warm.

Preheat a grill surface. Brush the tuna steaks with the remaining olive oil and season to taste with salt and black pepper.

Grill the tuna steaks to the desired doneness and serve topped with the prepared vinaigrette.

Serves 4

Herb and Almond Crusted Tuna Steak with Creole Aioli

4	7 ounce	tuna steak
1/2	stick	butter
	to taste	salt
	to taste	black pepper
1/4	cup	white flour
1/2	cup	almond, sliced and blanched
1	tablespoon	basil, chopped
1	tablespoon	garlic, chopped
1	tablespoon	rosemary, chopped
1	tablespoon	thyme, chopped
1	tablespoon	cilantro, chopped
1/2	portion	remoulade sauce (see page 40)
2	tablespoon	olive oil

Procedure: • Prepare the remoulade sauce and incorporate the olive oil.

Place the almonds, white flour and all of the herbs and seasonings in a food processor and blend well thoroughly.

Press both sides of the tuna steaks into the herb mixture. Melt the butter in a sauté pan. Sauté the herbed tuna steaks until brown on both sides and cooked to the desired doneness. Flip the steaks continuously to keep from burning the crust.

Serve the herbed tuna steaks with the Creole mustard aioli.

Serves 4

Grilled Tuna Steak with Salsa Verde

4	7 ounce	tuna steak
3/4	cup	olive oil
	to taste	salt
	to taste	black pepper
1/2	bunch	parsley, cleaned
2	clove	garlic
2	whole	anchovy
1	tablespoon	caper
1	tablespoon	red wine vinegar

Procedure:

- *Place the parsley, garlic, anchovies, capers, red wine vinegar and a 1/2 cup of the olive oil in a blender. Puree and season to taste with salt and black pepper.*

  Preheat a grill surface. Brush the tuna steaks with olive oil and season to taste with salt and black pepper.

  Grill the tuna steaks to the desired doneness and serve topped with the salsa verde.
  Serves 4

Sautéed Wahoo with Poached Oysters and Forestier Sauce

4	7 ounce	wahoo steak
1		egg
1/2	cup	milk
	to taste	salt
	to taste	white pepper
		white flour
1/2	cup	butter, melted
12	select	oyster
1/2	pound	mushroom, sliced
1	tablespoon	garlic, chopped
2	tablespoon	brandy
1	cup	red wine
1/2	cup	green onion, chopped
1	cup	Italian plum tomato, crushed
2	cup	veal stock
	to taste	black pepper, coarse ground

Procedure: • *In a sauce pot combine the red wine, brandy, tomatoes, veal stock, green onions, garlic and mushrooms.*

Reduce the sauce to half the original volume. Season to taste with salt and black pepper. Keep warm.

Blend the egg and milk together and season to taste with salt and white pepper.

Preheat a oven to 450˚. Dip the wahoo steaks in the milk wash. Dredge the fish through the white flour and shake off all of the excess flour.

Heat the melted butter in a sauté pan. Sauté the wahoo until brown on both sides. Transfer the sauté pan to the oven and bake the wahoo for 15 minutes.

Remove the wahoo from the oven and place the steaks on the base of 4 dinner plates.

Bring the reduced sauce to a slow boil. Add the oysters and cook until firm. Do not overcook the oysters.

Place 3 oysters on top of each wahoo steak and finish with the reduced forestier sauce.
Serves 4

Grilled Fish with Citrus Butter Sauce

4	7 ounce	fish filet, grilled
1	cup	heavy cream
1/2	cup	orange juice
1	tablespoon	lemon juice
2	tablespoon	lime juice
1	tablespoon	sugar
2	tablespoon	fish stock
2	stick	butter
	to taste	salt
	to taste	white pepper

Procedure:

- In a sauce pot, reduce the heavy cream, orange juice, lemon juice, lime juice, sugar and fish stock to half the original volume.

  Cut the butter into chips and whip into the reduced sauce until all of the butter is incorporated. Season to taste with salt and white pepper.

  Grill the fish filets that have been selected using the method described on page 165, grilled grouper.

  Serve the grilled filets topped with the citrus butter sauce.
  Serves 4

Grilled Triggerfish with Escarole and Roasted Peppers

4	7 ounce	triggerfish filet
		olive oil
	to taste	salt
	to taste	black pepper
1	portion	sautéed escarole (see page 76)
2	portion	roasted red sweet pepper (see page 50)
1/4	cup	balsamic vinegar
3	tablespoon	basil, chopped

Procedure:

- Prepare the roasted peppers.

  Preheat a grill surface. Brush the triggerfish with olive oil and season to taste with salt and black pepper.

  Grill the triggerfish filets until thoroughly cooked.

  Prepare the escarole and place on the base of 4 dinner plates. Place the grilled triggerfish filets on top of the sautéed escarole.

  Top the triggerfish filets with the roasted peppers and drizzle balsamic vinegar over each triggerfish filet.

  Garnish the triggerfish with chopped basil.
  Serves 4

Horseradish and Potato Crusted Salmon

4	7 ounce	salmon filet
3		egg yolk
2	tablespoon	horseradish
	to taste	salt
	to taste	black pepper
		white flour
2	large	Idaho potato
1	stick	butter
1	portion	Creole mustard aioli (see page 170)
1	tablespoon	dill, chopped

Procedure:

⬭ *Prepare the Creole mustard aioli.*

Blend the egg yolk and horseradish together.

Peel and grate the potatoes. Season the salmon filets to taste with salt and black pepper.

Coat the salmon filets with the egg mixture and then the grated potatoes.

Dust the salmon filets with white flour on both sides to absorb any excess moisture on the potatoes. Press the entire coating firmly against the salmon filets.

Preheat an oven to 400°. Melt the butter in a sauté pan and brown the salmon filets on one side.

Flip the salmon filets and transfer the sauté pan to the oven. Bake the salmon for 15 minutes. Check periodically so that the crust is not burning and flip the filets if necessary.

Remove the salmon filets from the oven and serve on 4 dinner plates topped with the prepared aioli.

Garnish with chopped dill.

Serves 4

Grilled Salmon with Rosemary Citrus Vinaigrette

4	7 ounce	salmon filet
1	cup	olive oil
	to taste	salt
	to taste	black pepper
1/4	cup	orange juice
2	tablespoon	lemon juice
2	tablespoon	lime juice
1	tablespoon	rice vinegar
2	tablespoon	chicken stock
2	tablespoon	rosemary, chopped

Procedure:

• Preheat a grill surface.

In a blender, combine 3/4 cup of olive oil with the rosemary, chicken stock, rice vinegar, lime juice, lemon juice and orange juice.

Blend the vinaigrette and season to taste with salt and black pepper.

Brush the salmon filets with the remaining olive oil and season to taste with salt and black pepper.

Grill the salmon filets until thoroughly cooked. Serve the grilled salmon filets on 4 dinner plates topped with the prepared citrus vinaigrette.

Serves 4

Grilled Jumbo Softshell Crabs

4	jumbo	softshell crab
1	portion	basil vinaigrette (see page 69)
		olive oil
	to taste	salt
	to taste	black pepper
1/4	cup	butter, melted
2	tablespoon	lemon juice
3	tablespoon	paprika
1/4	cup	green onion, chopped

Procedure: • *Prepare the basil vinaigrette.*

Preheat a grill surface. Preheat an oven to 450°.

Clean the softshell crabs by removing the lungs under the skin and trimming off the eyes and mouth.

Brush the crabs with olive oil and season to taste with salt and black pepper.

Place the crabs on the grill and mark both sides.

Transfer the crabs to a roasting pan and cover with the basil vinaigrette, butter, lemon juice, paprika and chopped green onions.

Bake for 10 minutes. Remove the crabs from the roasting pan and place on 4 dinner plates.

Reduce the pan drippings over a high fire until thick and serve over the softshell crabs.
Serves 4

Sautéed Jumbo Softshell Crabs with Garlic Meuniere Sauce

4	jumbo	softshell crab
1		egg
1/2	cup	milk
		white flour
	to taste	salt
	to taste	white pepper
1/2	cup	butter, melted
1	portion	meuniere sauce (see page 39)
2	tablespoon	garlic, chopped
	to taste	cayenne pepper
1/2	cup	green onion, chopped

Procedure: • *Clean the softshell crabs by removing the lungs underneath the skin and trimming off the eyes and mouth.*

Preheat an oven to 450˚. Prepare the meuniere sauce and add the garlic and cayenne pepper to taste. Keep warm.

Blend the egg and milk together and season to taste with salt and white pepper.

Dip the crabs in the milk wash. Dredge through the white flour and shake off all of the excess flour.

Heat the butter in a sauté pan and brown the crab on both sides. Transfer the sauté pan to the oven and bake for 10 minutes. Remove the crabs from the oven.

Place the crabs on 4 dinner plates and top with the prepared meuniere sauce. Garnish with chopped green onions.
Serves 4

Grilled Seafood Medley

4	3 ounce	fish filet
4	baby	softshell crab, cleaned
8	jumbo	shrimp, peeled
8	jumbo	sea scallop
2	Maine	lobster tail, steamed and split
1		gold sweet pepper, quartered
1		red sweet pepper, quartered
1		red onion, sliced
4		asparagus, steamed
		olive oil
	to taste	salt
	to taste	black pepper
1	portion	meuniere sauce (see page 39)
1/2	cup	green onion, chopped

Procedure: • *Prepare the meuniere sauce.*

Preheat a grill surface.

Brush all of the ingredients with olive oil and season to taste with salt and black pepper.

Place all of the ingredients on the grill in an order which allows the cooked items and vegetables to be finished the same time as the uncooked seafood items.

On 4 platters place 1 fish filet, 1 buster crab, 2 shrimp, 2 sea scallops, 1/2 a lobster tail, 1/4 piece of a red and gold pepper, 1 red onion slice and 1 asparagus spear.

Drizzle the meuniere sauce over all of the grilled items and garnish with chopped green onions.

Serves 4

Rosemary Shrimp

24	jumbo	shrimp
1/2	cup	olive oil
2	tablespoon	rosemary, chopped
1	tablespoon	garlic, chopped
1/2	cup	white wine
1/4	cup	lemon juice
1/2	cup	romano cheese, grated
	to taste	black pepper

Procedure:

• Peel the shrimp and cut a shallow split in the top center of the shrimp running from head to tail.

Heat the olive oil in a sauté pan. Add the shrimp and sauté for 3 minutes.

Add the rosemary and garlic and cook for an additional minute. Add the white wine and lemon juice and cook for an additional 2 minutes.

Add the grated romano cheese and remove from the fire. Toss until all of the cheese is incorporated. Season to taste with black pepper.

Serves 4

Grilled Shrimp with Cilantro Cream and Sweet Pepper Salsa

24	jumbo	shrimp
		olive oil
	to taste	salt
	to taste	black pepper
2		red sweet pepper, roasted and diced (see page 50)
1	portion	pico de gallo (see page 30)
4	portion	cilantro cream (see page 80)

Procedure:

● Prepare the pico de gallo and add the diced roasted red pepper.

Prepare the cilantro cream.

Preheat a grill surface. Peel the shrimp and cut a shallow split in the top center of the shrimp running from head to tail.

Brush the shrimp with olive oil and season to taste with salt and black pepper.

Grill the shrimp until thoroughly cooked. Remove from the grill and keep warm.

Place the cilantro cream on the base of 4 dinner plates and arrange the shrimp on top of the cream. Garnish with a 2 ounce portion of the roasted sweet pepper salsa.

Serves 4

Spiced Scallops Braised in Corn Infused Olive Oil

24	jumbo	sea scallop
1/2	cup	cumin
3/4	cup	chili powder
1	cup	olive oil
1	can	corn
1	tablespoon	garlic, chopped
	to taste	salt
	to taste	white pepper
1		tomato, diced
1/4	cup	cilantro, chopped
1	tablespoon	lime juice

Procedure: • In a blender, puree the corn with liquid, olive oil and garlic until very smooth.

In a sauce pot, bring the pureed mixture to a slow boil for 15 minutes. Season to taste with salt and white pepper. Strain through a chinois or china cap.

Blend the cumin and chili powder. Roll the scallops in this mixture.

In a sauté pan, heat the corn oil. Add the scallops and sauté for 5 minutes.

Add the lime juice and transfer the scallops to 4 dinner plates. Serve the scallops garnished with the diced tomato and chopped cilantro.
Serves 4

Steamed Maine Lobster

4	1 1/2 pound	Maine lobster, live
4		lemon
1	cup	butter, melted

Procedure: • Fill a 4 gallon pot with hot water 6 inches from the top and bring to a high rolling boil.

Melt the butter and keep warm.

Cut the lemons in half.

Place the lobsters in the boiling water and cook until the lobsters float to the top of the water. Remove the lobsters from the water.

Break off the tails and split the bottom of the shell from tip to tail.

With the back edge of a knife crack the claws across the center on both sides.

Reassemble the lobsters on 4 platters and serve with lemons and melted butter.

(Freeze the shells and heads to make lobster stock.)
Serves 4

Chilled Stone Crab Claws with Hot Mustard

16		stone crab claw, steamed and chilled
1	cup	mayonnaise
1/2	cup	Dijon®mustard
1	tablespoon	lemon juice
	to taste	cayenne pepper

Procedure:

■ *Blend the mayonnaise, Dijon®mustard, lemon juice and cayenne pepper to taste in a mixing bowl.*

Crack the stone crab claws and serve with the hot mustard.
Serves 4

Mussels Steamed in Red Sauce

80		mussel, cleaned
2	portion	marinara sauce (see page 42)
1	cup	white wine
	to taste	crushed red pepper

Procedure:

■ *In a large sauté pan bring the white wine to a boil. Add the mussels and cover.*

Steam for 3 minutes. Add the marinara sauce and crushed red pepper to taste. Return the cover.

Cook until all of the mussels have opened. Serve immediately.
Serves 4

Desserts

Some peoples' view of a great meal is directly proportional to their enjoyment of the dessert course. My suggestion then, order dessert first. If it's good, ask your waiter for a menu, if it's not, request the check and some coffee. Seriously, dessert is often overlooked in restaurants as well as on the homefront.

I mentioned earlier that the appetizer course is a great introduction to the meal and a preview of the wonderful food yet to come. I feel certain such a great first impression will be lost if the closing statement to a fine meal is frozen, store-bought and cool-whipped.

Desserts can be elegant, either simple with the right accompaniments or complex, such as fresh berries with English cream or utilizing baked flourless chocolate cakes with raspberry sauce and espresso cream or a crisp almond tulip cup with your choice of fillings. The great thing about most desserts is that they can be prepared in advance and take a minimal amount of time to assemble and serve, leaving the cook free to concentrate on hot food preparation.

I can only predict that this may be the section in your book that develops a crease in the binding and simply pops open when in hand.

Corleone

12	scoop	vanilla ice cream
1	cup	almond, sliced and blanched
1/4	cup	pecan, shelled
1/2	cup	white chocolate, chopped
1/2	cup	dark chocolate, chopped
1	tablespoon	cinnamon
2	teaspoon	nutmeg
3/4	cup	graham cracker crumb
2	cup	honey
		fresh mint

Requested by
BON APPÉTIT magazine

Procedure:

• *Blend all of the ingredients except the honey, ice cream and mint in a food processor. Chop until a fine texture is achieved.*

Roll each scoop of vanilla ice cream in the Corleone mixture until completely coated.

Serve the Corleones in wine glasses topped with honey and garnish with fresh mint.
Serves 12

Belgian Chocolate Mousse

20		egg white
2	cup	sugar
5	ounce	semi-sweet chocolate
4	tablespoon	butter

Procedure:

• *Melt the butter and chocolate together over a double boiler.*

Whip the egg whites, slowly adding all of the sugar. Whip until firm peaks form.

Fold in the butter and chocolate mixture slowly. Refrigerate for 2 hours and serve in wine glasses.
Serves 12

Pecan Pie

1	stick	butter, melted
1	cup	light corn syrup
1	cup	sugar
3	large	egg, beaten
1	teaspoon	lemon juice
1	teaspoon	vanilla
1	pinch	salt
1 1/4	cup	pecan, chopped

• Crust

4	cup	white flour
2		egg
2		egg yolk
2/3	cup	sugar
1	pound	butter, chipped
1/3	teaspoon	salt

Procedures:

• Crust

Blend all of the ingredients together. Mix by hand until all of the butter is incorporated and the dough is smooth.

Roll the dough until the desired thickness is achieved. Roll the dough onto the rolling pin and unroll over a 12 inch tart pan.

Press the dough into the tart pan and cut the excess dough off the edges. Chill.

Preheat an oven to 375°.

• Pie Filling

Blend all of the ingredients in a mixing bowl.

Pour the mixture into the chilled pie shell. Transfer the pie to the oven and bake for 25 minutes.

Remove the pie from the oven and let stand 15 minutes before slicing to serve.

Serves 8

Raisin Banana Bread Pudding

1	stale	French bread loaf (3 feet long)
2		banana, peeled and chopped
1	cup	raisin
4		egg
3	cup	half and half
1	tablespoon	vanilla
1	cup	sugar
1	stick	butter, chipped
1	portion	English cream (see page 188)
2	ounce	cream de banana liqueur

Requested by GOURMET magazine

Procedure:

● *Prepare the English cream and add the banana liqueur.*

Blend the eggs, half and half, vanilla and sugar in a mixing bowl.

Preheat an oven to 350°.

Cut the stale bread into bite size pieces and place in a 9x12x2 inch pan.

Add the bananas, raisins and butter. Pour the half and half mixture over the bread mixture and blend in thoroughly.

Place the bread pudding in the oven and bake for 35 minutes. Cover the bread pudding with aluminum foil if the bread pudding begins to brown too quickly.

Remove the bread pudding from the oven and let stand for 10 minutes before serving.

Serve the bread pudding in bowls topped with the prepared banana flavored English cream.

Serves 8

English Cream

8		egg yolk
1/2	cup	sugar
1	tablespoon	vanilla
2	cup	heavy cream

Procedure:

▪ *In a sauce pot, bring the heavy cream to a slow boil.*

In a mixing bowl, combine all of the remaining ingredients and blend thoroughly.

Add one cup of the heated cream to the mixing bowl stirring continuously. Pour this mixture back into the sauce pot with the remaining cup of cream.

Stir this mixture continuously until steaming. Do not boil. Remove from the fire and chill.
Serves 8

Banana Cream Crepe

1/2	cup	white flour
2		egg
3	tablespoon	sugar
	pinch	salt
1/4	cup	heavy cream
1	ounce	brandy
1/2	cup	milk
3	tablespoon	butter, melted
1/2	cup	powdered sugar
		mint leaf

▪ *Banana Cream*

2	cup	heavy cream
3/4	cup	sugar
2		banana, peeled and pureed

Procedures:

▪ *Banana Cream*
Combine the heavy cream and sugar in a mixing bowl and whip until firm peaks form. Fold in the pureed bananas and chill.

• Crepe

Combine the eggs, white flour, sugar and salt in a mixing bowl and blend thoroughly.

Slowly incorporate the heavy cream, milk, brandy and butter stirring continuously.

Heat a 12 inch non stick sauté pan on a medium fire. Place 2 ounces of the crepe batter in the center of the sauté pan and swirl to coat the entire bottom of the pan. (If the batter bubbles immediately, the pan is too hot.)

Allow the crepe to brown on the edges. Flip the crepe and cook for 15 seconds. Remove the crepe from the pan and continue this process until all of the crepe batter has been used.

Place the crepes on dessert plates. Place 1/3 cup of the banana cream in the center of the crepe and fold the crepe into triangles or circular tubes.

Serve garnished with powdered sugar and fresh mint.

Serves 6

Banana Walnut Spice Cake

1	cup	walnut, chopped coarse
2	cup	white flour
2	teaspoon	baking soda
1/2	teaspoon	salt
1/2	teaspoon	nutmeg
1/2	teaspoon	cinnamon
1/2	teaspoon	clove
1/4	teaspoon	mace
2	cup	sugar
1	cup	vegetable oil
2		egg
4		banana, peeled and sliced thin

Recipe by
Pastry Chef Tui Cassube

Procedure: ☒ Preheat an oven to 350°.

Butter and flour a 10x3 inch springform pan.

In a mixing bowl sift together the flour, baking soda, salt, nutmeg, cinnamon, cloves and mace. Set aside.

In a mixing bowl, using an electric mixer, beat the sugar and vegetable oil for 5 minutes. Add the eggs 1 at a time, beating thoroughly after each addition.

Add all of the dry ingredients and stir until thoroughly mixed. This batter will be very thick.

Stir in the bananas and walnuts until thoroughly mixed.

Pour this mixture into the springform pan and place in the pre-heated oven.

Bake for 1 1/2 hours or until a knife inserted into the center of the cake comes out clean and dry. Remove and transfer to a cooling rack for 15 minutes.

Remove the cake from the pan. Slice and serve warm with your favorite ice cream.
Serves 12

White Chocolate Banana Cream Pie

1	portion	tart shell crust (see page 186)
3	portion	banana cream (see page 188)
3		banana, peeled and thinly sliced
2	cup	white chocolate, grated fine
		nutmeg

Procedure: ☒ Prepare the tart shell and bake in a 375° oven until brown. Remove the crust from the oven and allow to cool completely.

Prepare the banana cream and chill.

Line the bottom of the crust with sliced bananas. Pour the banana cream into the shell. Start the cream in a high mound in the center of the pie and slope it gradually to meet the edges.

Cover the pie with the grated chocolate and garnish with nutmeg.
Serves 12

Chocolate Éclairs

1	cup	water
1/2	stick	butter
1/4	teaspoon	salt
1	cup	flour
4	large	egg
2		egg yolk
1	tablespoon	water

⊡ Pastry Cream

2	cup	milk
6		egg yolk
2/3	cup	sugar
1	teaspoon	vanilla
1/2	cup	flour
3/4	cup	dark chocolate, melted

Procedures:

⊡ Pastry Cream

Bring the milk to a slow boil in a sauce pot.

Blend all of the remaining ingredients in a mixing bowl. Add this mixture to the heated milk.

Bring to a slow boil stirring continuously. Remove from the heat and chill.

⊡ Éclair Shells

In a sauce pot, bring the water, butter and salt to a boil.

Stir in the flour until all is incorporated and remove from the heat.

Add the whole eggs one at a time completely incorporating each egg before adding the next.

Preheat an oven to 350°.

Place the batter in a pastry bag with no tip and pipe a 1 inch wide strip 3 1/2 inches long onto a buttered and floured cookie sheet.

Blend the 2 egg yolks with the water and brush the top of each piped shell.

• *Place the éclair shells in the oven and bake for 25 minutes. Be certain that the shells are brown and have a dry, hollow feeling before removing from the oven. Let cool.*

Pierce a small hole in one end of the éclair shells.

Place the pastry cream in a pastry bag with a small round tip and pipe the cream into the éclair shells.

Be certain that the cream has traveled to the opposite side of the shells. If it has not pierce a small hole in the opposite side and repeat the above procedure.

Repeat this process until all of the shells have been filled.
Serves 10

Berries with Citrus Cream

1	pint	berry
2	cup	heavy cream
1/2	cup	sugar
1		lime, zest and juice
1		lemon, zest and juice
1		orange, zest and juice
2	tablespoon	Grand Marnier
		mint leaf

Procedure: • *Whip the heavy cream and sugar until stiff peaks form.*

Fold the fruit juices, zest and Grand Marnier into the cream mixture. Chill.

Fold a pint of fresh berries into the cream mixture and serve in wine glasses. Garnish with mint leaves.
Serves 6

Bananas Foster

1/2	stick	butter
1/4	cup	brown sugar
1	tablespoon	vanilla
1	ounce	brandy
1	ounce	Grand Marnier
1/2	cup	creme de banana
1	dash	lemon juice
4		banana, peeled and sliced (1/2 inch thick)
1/4	cup	almond, toasted and chopped
6	scoop	vanilla ice cream

Procedure:

☐ *Melt the butter in a large sauté pan.*

Add all of the remaining ingredients except the ice cream and almonds. Flambe and cook for 2 minutes. (Be cautious of the alcohol igniting instantly if using a gas range.)

Place the vanilla ice cream in wine glasses and top with the sautéed mixture. Garnish with the chopped almonds.

Serves 6

Key Lime Cheesecake

6		egg
1	cup	butter, melted
2	cup	sugar
2	tablespoon	vanilla
2	pound	cream cheese
1	ounce	white creme de cacao
1/4	cup	key lime juice

☐ *Crust*

3/4	cup	graham cracker crumb
1/4	cup	sugar
1/3	cup	butter, melted

Procedures:

■ *Crust*
Preheat an oven to 325°.

Blend all of the ingredients together in a mixing bowl. Press into the bottom of a 10x3 inch springform pan.

Place the crust in the oven and bake until the edges are brown. Remove from the oven and allow to cool.

■ *Cheesecake*
Soften the cream cheese. Place all of the ingredients in a mixer with a wire whip attachment.

Whip on medium speed until the batter is smooth and there are no cream cheese lumps.

Pour this mixture into the springform pan. Place the cake in the oven and cook for 20 minutes.

Reduce the temperature to 250°. Cook for 30 minutes or until the center is firm to the touch.

Turn off the oven and allow the cake to cool in the oven with the door closed for 20 minutes.

Refrigerate for 4 hours. Slice and serve.
Serves 12

Tirami-Su

10		egg yolk
1	cup	sugar
1/4	cup	rum
1	pound	mascarpone cheese
4		egg white
2	cup	heavy cream
2	sheet	sponge cake (12x16x1/4 inch)
3	cup	espresso coffee, cold
1/4	cup	cocoa powder

Procedure: • Beat the egg yolks with 3/4 cup sugar until thick. Add the rum and set aside.

Whip the mascarpone cheese until smooth and fold into the whipped egg yolks

Whip the egg whites with the remaining sugar until firm peaks form.

Whip the heavy cream until firm peaks form.

Fold the egg whites and cream into the mascarpone cheese mixture.

Place one sheet of the sponge cake on a cookie sheet. Soak the spongecake with 11/2 cup of espresso.

Pour half of the cheese cream mixture over the espresso soaked spongecake. Chill for 20 minutes.

Place the second spongecake on top of the cheese cream mixture.

Repeat the above procedure with the espresso and cheese cream mixture. Refrigerate for 4 hours.

Dust the top of the tirami-su with cocoa powder shortly before serving.
Serves 16

Index

Index

Chef Tim Creehan's
Flavors of the Gulf Coast Cookbook
c/o Creehan's Market
P.O. Box 1504, Destin, FL 32540

Please send _____**copy(ies)**   @ $ 19.00 each _____ (Tax Included)
       2 day postage and handling   @ $ 3.50 each _____
                                             TOTAL [   ]

Name _____

Address _____

City _____ State _____ Zip _____

Make checks payable to: Creehan's Market ■

Chef Tim Creehan's
Flavors of the Gulf Coast Cookbook
c/o Creehan's Market
P.O. Box 1504, Destin, FL 32540

Please send _____**copy(ies)**   @ $ 19.00 each _____ (Tax Included)
       2 day postage and handling   @ $ 3.50 each _____
                                             TOTAL [   ]

Name _____

Address _____

City _____ State _____ Zip _____

Make checks payable to: Creehan's Market ■

Chef Tim Creehan's
Flavors of the Gulf Coast Cookbook
c/o Creehan's Market
P.O. Box 1504, Destin, FL 32540

Please send _____**copy(ies)**   @ $ 19.00 each _____ (Tax Included)
       2 day postage and handling   @ $ 3.50 each _____
                                             TOTAL [   ]

Name _____

Address _____

City _____ State _____ Zip _____

Make checks payable to: Creehan's Market ■

I want to Brush it on! with Chef Tim Creehan's

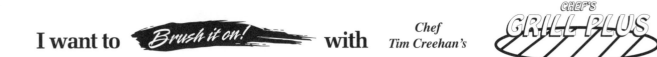

Please send me: (7 oz)	Quantity	Price (with tax)	Subtotal
Original Flavor		$3.00	
Lemon Pepper		$3.00	
Fiery Hot Habanero		$3.00	
Mesquite Grill		$3.00	
(Shipping & Handling)	1 -3 Units	$5.95	
	4 -7 Units	$8.95	
	8 + Units	$12.95	

Name

Address

City

State

Zip

Phone

E-mail

Total Due:

For a *free* sample of **Chef's Grill Plus,**® check us out on our web page at www.grillplus.com
Questions or comments?
Call our toll free number: 1-888-457-4735
E-mail us: info@grillplus.com

Send order form to: P.O. Box 1504 • Destin • FL 32540 • Make check payable to: **Creehan's Market**

I want to Brush it on! with Chef Tim Creehan's

Please send me: (7 oz)	Quantity	Price (with tax)	Subtotal
Original Flavor		$3.00	
Lemon Pepper		$3.00	
Fiery Hot Habanero		$3.00	
Mesquite Grill		$3.00	
(Shipping & Handling)	1 -3 Units	$5.95	
	4 -7 Units	$8.95	
	8 + Units	$12.95	

Name

Address

City

State

Zip

Phone

E-mail

Total Due:

For a *free* sample of **Chef's Grill Plus,**® check us out on our web page at www.grillplus.com
Questions or comments?
Call our toll free number: 1-888-457-4735
E-mail us: info@grillplus.com

Send order form to: P.O. Box 1504 • Destin • FL 32540 • Make check payable to: **Creehan's Market**